LISTENING IN

A RECORD OF A SINGULAR EXPERIENCE

By

OLIVE C.B. PIXLEY

Copyright
The Armour of Light Trust Council

Revised Publication 1999

ISBN 0 9536630 1 9

Published by
The Armour of Light Trust Council

Copyright © Olive C.B. Pixley
All rights reserved. No part of this publication
may be reproduced, stored in a retrieval system,
or transmitted, in any form or by any means,
electronic or otherwise,
without the prior permission of
The Amour of Light Trust Council.
This book is sold subject to the condition that
it shall not, by way of trade or otherwise,
be lent, resold, hired out, or otherwise circulated
without the prior consent of The Amour of Light Trust Council
in any form of binding or cover other than that in which it is published,
and without a similar condition, including this condition,
being imposed on the subsequent purchaser.

Printed by
Waveney Print
College Lane, Worlingham, Beccles, Suffolk NR34 7SA

TO JACK

You, when alive,
Did realize that life was wondrous fair,
Held nothing worth that others could not share,
Lived but to give.

Death, sure and swift,
A wholly conscious sacrifice from you,
For you loved life — it was your rightful due —
And then, your gift.

With you we die
To that which death can touch. With you we live
Always. That Love and Wisdom may perceive
The reason WHY?

O.C.B.P.

November, 1917

PREFACE

It seems necessary to me to preface the following narrative with an apology, for it has taken me ten years to realize that my duty towards my neighbour includes the sharing of an intimate personal experience.

What has been a pleasure to tell, is an effort to write, for I have a real dislike of adding to the unnecessary literature of the world. It may be old-fashioned, but I have a conviction that privacy of thought and action is a precious possession of the over-exposed condition of our modern existence.

I have never cared, and do not care now, whether the following facts are believed or not. If the narrative be true, then those who read it will be glad one day of their knowledge. If it be a phantasy, no one suffers.

So I write it, not for the scientist, to whom I can prove nothing, nor for the intelligent sceptic, for whom other people's experiences are valueless, but for all those who, like myself, have lost the dearest of companions - the vital focus of their lives - around whom all thought and action centred. For those alone I write, in the hope that they too may share my realization, that life neither begins nor ends here, and that the transition from one state of existence to another is the most radiant and joyous adventure.

O.C.B.P
Wooburn House
Bucks.

February 1928

LISTENING IN

I

It is not possible to tell the following story and eliminate the personal element. The tiresome reiteration of the word "I" is, I fear, inevitable.

I must start by being biographical, so that you may know the sort of people my brother and I were, and exactly how it all happened.

When we grew up, we became inseparable companions, and discovered that we both possessed a certain amount of psychic ability, which in those long ago pre-war days, manifested itself in automatic writing. We satisfied ourselves by certain tests that it was not our subconscious minds operating, but my brother was frankly frightened of it. Curiously enough, he was encouraged to write by those controlling his hand; I, on the contrary, was always warned against it. When we pressed for an explanation, "they" wrote that as a small boy he had come in contact with evil and had overcome it and was therefore immune, and that I had not and was therefore vulnerable.

We then asked what "they" referred to, and my brother was reminded of a terrifying experience he had had when quite a small boy at his first private school.

It occurred one Sunday afternoon in the winter. The house was an old one with long dark passages. All the boys were assembled in the headmaster's study and had been told to bring their Bibles. Jack had forgotten his and was sent to his classroom to fetch it. The long passages were quite dark - whether they should have been lit I do not know - anyhow, my brother ran very hurriedly along and found his Bible, and when recalling the story, he told me what an appalling sense of fear came over him as he got to the door and had to face the gloomy corridor again.

He darted forward and felt a cord around his neck - something thin, strong and flexible. He screamed and put up his hands to break it. He couldn't. He struggled with the invisible wire all down the passage and fell at the end.

When he did not return, the master went to look for him and found him lying unconscious, with a thin red line on his neck and across the palms of both hands. Strict investigations were made, and it was proved to be no practical joke played by boy or servant and the incident could never be explained. No fragments of string or wire were ever found, nor was it possible for anything to have been attached to the walls outside the classroom door. The fact that he had reached the room safely and that the terrifying thing had happened on the return journey, made it extraordinarily difficult to suggest a possible solution. The incident was hushed up and not discussed. It was not advisable for domestic reasons - and for the health of small boys - to dwell on the possibility of a supernormal manifestation. My brother never forgot the horror of that experience, and said that the wire felt alive and he struggled as though he were fighting for his life, and as he broke it he fainted - but that he knew he had broken it first.

It was a curious experience for a child to have, and my brother was impressed when "they" reminded him of it so many years after, when the affair had completely gone out of his mind. We accepted "their" interpretation of it, and after that he always held the pencil when we tried the writing together.

When Jack left Oxford he had visions of becoming an architect, and to that end started work in a well-known architect's office. In the meantime an Oxford friend had been prospecting in Kenya, then known as British East Africa. He returned full of enthusiasm and confident that a vast fortune awaited the enterprising settler.

Architecture was abandoned, and Jack and his friend entered into partnership and sailed for B.E.A. It was understood between us that I should join him in a year's time and keep house for him.

How seldom do the golden visions of youth ever materialize!

In answer to one of my letters in which I had asked him if he ever tried the writing, and if so with what result, he wrote - "B.E.A. is the most 'unpsychic' place. I never feel I want to - and never do."

He was coming home for Christmas the year war broke out, but he immediately enlisted in the King's African Rifles and saw a good deal of fighting out there.

Like all the rest, he had a longing to be in the thick of it on the Western Front, so he returned to England and was given a commission in the Grenadier Guards.

He had bad bouts of fever which delayed his training at Chelsea, and during all those months I was working in London and saw him daily.

Jack had an extraordinarily sympathetic, understanding nature, and was intensely interested in people. He adored life and had the most vital personality I had ever known. I have noticed the mental atmosphere of a room full of people change completely when he entered - it became re-charged, re-vitalized by his presence.

He never worried, never looked ahead. He lived each day to the full and fervently hoped he would live till he was ninety. Personally, I thought twenty-five was an ideal age to die.

He never thought he would be killed - nor did I. We often discussed how and when he would be wounded. Then on the last night of his last leave he said to me suddenly, "You know if anything does happen to me, I don't want a memorial service. They are so dreary and I'd hate mother to go to it." I acquiesced, with no shadow of fore-warning and with no premonition. Our farewell that early morning, on the doorstep of the house of a mutual friend with whom we were both staying, was gay - almost casual - I wouldn't face the possibility of anything happening. His wonderful luck must hold to the end. It did. He went off to the crowd and bustle of the leave train at Victoria - (that, I could not face) - and we were left behind - eagerly planning for his next leave.

II.

A week later, on October 12th, 1917, Jack was shot by a sniper, straight through the heart. He was commanding a company, and after coming safely through a terrible engagement had just gone to look after his men......

My mother and I were at Harrogate for reasons of health. To my intense annoyance the doctor had told me to take several months' complete rest. I was due in France to work for the F.W.E.F. (French Wounded Emergency Fund) the following week. I wanted so much to be in France while Jack was there and thought Amiens might possibly be a meeting place for short leaves.

The doctor insisted on my cancelling this arrangement the day before the telegram came. Little did I realize in my bitter disappointment what a good turn the doctor was doing me.

The telegram was telephoned through and my mother and I returned home the same day. That was a Monday. On the following Thursday I was having breakfast in bed, with a bad cold. I was crying - hopelessly - and saying out loud, "Jack, Jack." Suddenly in my head, I heard him say - "Yes, I'm here." I stopped crying, sat erect suddenly, upsetting my tray, and said, "Jack, is that you?" Again he said, "Yes, I'm here, sitting on the end of your bed." It was unbelievably true - I couldn't see him but he repeated again and again that it was he himself and that he was just going to the dining-room to see the others, who were having breakfast. There was a pause while I sat dazed and incredulous, and then in a few minutes he returned, told me exactly where they were all sitting, *what they were talking about* and other details, all of which I verified later.

I must try to explain here how the process of communication was carried on by my brother and me. He used my head and mouth, and at first with great force, so that my head jerked with every word he uttered. Later on he found he could do it more easily by using less force, and then my head hardly moved. Sometimes I spoke the words out loud - as if they were forced out of me by every jerk of the head, afterwards it was the same articulation that one uses when one is learning poetry, silently, by heart.

I always felt him at my right side. I could never lie down and talk to him. I instinctively felt I must sit up and have my right side free.

I never knew when he was coming - I never called him, but I always knew the instant he was there. A terribly poignant feeling would always overwhelm me so that I had to cry. Normally I find it hard to cry and resent intensely being forced to shed tears - but I realize now the safeguard it was - for no one trying to impersonate my brother could arouse such emotion in me. Before he started speaking I would feel his unseen presence and the tears would start, often most inconveniently.

Once he came when I was sitting in a packed third-class compartment, leaving Paddington. Before I could do anything, the tears were crowding down my cheeks. Fortunately at that moment the air-raid signals crashed out and we were instantly plunged into darkness and I could cry in peace! I thought for one joyful moment we were going to be blown up and that Jack had come for me.   Not at all. He had come hastily to tell me that a miniature of him which was being painted for me, and in the execution of which I had asked him to inspire the artist to produce a good likeness, was finished, and that he thought it was very good. The following morning I got a letter from a friend who was giving me the miniature, telling me that it was finished, that it pleased him and that he thought it an excellent likeness.

III.

That, then, was the way it started, and it never varied. I never knew when he was coming, or for how long he would stay. Quite suddenly he would say, "I must go now." I would urge him to stop, but he never did. It always seemed as if he withdrew as he repeated quite slowly, "I . . . must . . . go . . . now." I would say "Good-bye Jack," and he would answer quickly "Never that word." He never would let me say "good-bye." It dropped out so often and so unconsciously, and yet every time he pulled me up. "Adieu" - any other word, but never "good-bye."

I can't, of course, convey to you the marvel of those conversations. It lay in his utter naturalness and the unexpectedness of his answers to my incessant questions. He was thrilled by his conditions, and therefore he had taken great trouble to find out how he could communicate with me in such a manner that I should know without a shadow of doubt that it was he.

Jack knew well by past experience how sceptical I was of communications purporting to come from well-known people. He realized I should never try to write, for I should never be able to convince myself that anything he wrote through me was not my own longing, finding automatic expression. When I asked him how he had discovered that he could talk through me, he mentioned the name of a friend in the same regiment and said that he had shown him how to do it, and that it had been pure experiment on his part as he did not know if it would succeed. But undoubtedly our minds had always vibrated to the same wavelength; often in the old days I knew what Jack was going to say before he spoke, and he had the same intuitive sensitiveness in regard to me; we used to have amusing moments when we found speech wasn't necessary for either of us. Now it was the more intensely interesting, as I could not know or visualize even what he was seeing. Often I had to wait before he answered, as he was so afraid of giving me the wrong impression. Sometimes I waited so long that I had to say, as if I were telephoning,

Listening In

"Jack, are you there?"

    My brother had an intense love of beauty and instinctive good taste. He adored nature and animals and was pagan in outlook in that Pan as a deity of natural phantasy appealed to him. The worship of God in churches seemed confined and dreary to him, so that I was astonished when he suddenly came to me as I was walking in the garden and said, "Olive, I want a memorial service." I said, "Do you remember what you said about them?" and he answered, "Yes, but I never knew what prayer was until I came here. It is *the* force that operates in my world, as electricity does in yours. Prayer materially alters our conditions; when you pray for those who have passed on, it is like giving them presents, you alter conditions that can *only* be changed by the force of prayer." He told me not to do anything more then but that he would let me know when he wanted it. He was killed on October 12th, and it was not until just before Christmas that he suddenly came and said he wanted his memorial service on December 28th. Most of the time I had forgotten he had ever wanted one, and now it seemed to me unnecessary.

    Jack was very insistent about it. He said it was a very important day for him and gave me detailed instructions. He wanted it at St. Martin-in-the-Fields at 1 o'clock. We went to London the same day and made arrangements and put it in the papers. We could not help what people would think about having a memorial service for him more than two months after: it was *his* memorial service, and he had arranged it. We left it at that. As a matter of fact many of his friends turned up at that service who were over from France on leave - which we could not have known. Jack told me afterwards that we should never know here what that service had accomplished for him. It was a very important time for him and all our prayers had achieved a definite result.

IV.

I must try to tell you his first impressions when he found much to his surprise and dismay that he could not continue the life on earth he so loved.

It was because the whole procedure was such a complete surprise to him that he just had to share it with us.

First, then, the beauty of his immediate surroundings impressed him enormously, "more-like-the-Russian-Ballet." (Which we had both so enjoyed together on its first appearance in London.) "More-like-the-Arabian-Night's Tales." How difficult he found it to give me anything like an adequate picture! The colour, light, vitality of it all delighted him. He was never tired, always exhilarated. Day and night do not exist, but periods in time are important. Dawn is the most important time on our earth. His world and ours touch at dawn. During that first Lent he used to wake me up at dawn so that I should talk to him and learn to get in touch with the vibrations of both worlds.

That was the greatest effort of them all - the spirit is willing - but the flesh is most grievously weak. I am ashamed to remember the awful effort it was, not only to wake, but to keep awake and not to turn on my side and go cosily to sleep again. But Jack knew that he was laying a foundation for knowledge that I could apprehend in no other way. He persevered, and by Easter - that most wonderful time for them and for us - he achieved his object. The instrument was now less blunt and could register more accurately.

A condition which he disliked very much at first, but afterwards became so used to that he never even referred to it again, was - "Everything that is inside in your world is outside here, and," said Jack, "I hate it." When I ask him what he meant, he explained that all our thoughts that we can keep to ourselves as our own possessions are *outside* with them. When they come in contact with each other they know their thoughts. It is not possible for them to think one thing and say

Listening In

another. Jack found it intolerable when he realized his powerlessness to keep himself to himself. His annoyance, however, soon wore off and he adapted himself to his new conditions in the same way as one adopts the recognized customs of any strange country one may find oneself in.

He then told me that every house in this side has also an emanation there; and when I asked him where he was living, he replied, "In the country with four friends." I asked him whether he was living in the emanation of our home here, and he said "No," and when I wanted to know who was, he told me that he did not know. "Can't you see now?" I asked. "Certainly not," he replied. He then explained that there is privacy there, and that if he were to try to look into the house, it would be on a par with our looking through a keyhole, and that it simply wasn't done. I had taken it for granted that, because they could not keep their thoughts to themselves, neither would they be allowed to live private lives.

There are, it appears, trees and buildings in *form* the same as ours, only far more beautiful and chemically absolutely different. Jack said it was ridiculous to think form only existed in our world when the fact was that our most beautiful works of art are the result of inspiration from the forms of their world. They have a colour there which we have not here (as yet). He tried to give me the name of it, but I couldn't get it, for it conveyed nothing to my mind and he had not the words to describe it.

I asked if he had seen any Germans. I wanted to know whether, in those early days, he had been back again in Flanders. He said, "No." If you were not a soldier you did not have to go back to help. Jack had hated war and all the conditions of warfare; he had been intensely proud of his regiment and of his company, but at heart he was an artist, not a soldier, and his work on the other side was therefore not connected with the battle front. Apparently, directly he had adjusted himself to his new surroundings, his work lay in trying to make those who had passed on as suddenly as he had appreciate the beauty of their condition.

Emphatically he assured me that they keep their own individuality, for death alters nothing, except the chemical conditions of the body, and leaves the mind precisely the same. The limitations of the physical form are removed and exchanged for the capacities of ethereal conditions and the readjustment is entirely a mental and spiritual one.

No allowance in this world or the next is made for ignorance. No ignorant person here is saved from being burnt if they put their hand in the fire. We can always learn if we want to. "Ye have not, because ye ask not." "Seek, and ye shall find."

Jack always had an intense power of appreciation and a very generous nature. He had that rare gift of kindling enthusiasm, and, once convinced of a thing, he would find no difficulty in making others see it from his point of view, though they might have taken a very long time to apprehend it on their own account. He enjoyed his work and it was one very well suited to his particular gifts.

V.

When he first went over he only saw people he cared for. *Love is the only Link.* You cannot get in touch with anybody except through love. That opens a pretty wide field to our imagination as to the radiant conditions existing there.

We have no power here to inflict suffering on those who pass on. Whatever we do or leave undone, we cannot cause them pain. All the ghostly visitations that occur are never to alter the ways of the living, but to try to repair some omission occasioned by their unexpected death. By prayer alone can we help them. They have the power of looking forward in time, and we can only look back, so as they see the ultimate issue of things; we cannot hurt them by any error of judgement.

Listening In

    Naturally, when I knew that Jack could look forward and see ahead, I implored him to tell me certain personal things I very much wanted to know. But he said, "Don't ask me, I mustn't tell you anything that will affect your judgement." I knew he was longing to tell me, but I also sensed that he did not want me to press him, as the right thing for both of us was that he should not tell - and he never has.

    A favourite walk of ours was an herbaceous bordered path by the side of a small river that runs through the grounds. One day he was telling me about certain conditions foretold by the Bible (and of which I will tell you later). I was enthralled, and at the same time remembering, with a constriction of the heart, the many times we had walked that path together, discussing amusing and mundane things. Quite unconsciously I kept on answering and saying - "Yes, darling," and then again in a few minutes, "Yes, darling," to show him I was understanding it all. Suddenly, so quickly that it was literally as startling as a slap in the face, he said - "I'm not 'darling'. I'm still Jack!" He knew, and I realized at once that if he had been walking in the flesh along that path, I should not have called him "darling" so incessantly. Therefore he would not allow me to alter in any respect my intimate knowledge of his indestructible personality. He is still "Jack".

VI.

He talked to me every day for about a fortnight, and then silence.

I did not know if he was ever coming back. I could do nothing, but by then I had utter confidence in his power that if it were possible for him, I knew he would return. I also felt strongly that I must not do anything to force what had been a perfectly spontaneous act on his part.

One evening three weeks later, when I was dressing for dinner, he suddenly returned. It was exactly as if he were walking up and down in my room, as he said so emphatically, "I cannot understand why I did not think of these things before." Then he explained. Like everyone who passes over, he had been through the whole of his past life, re-living in every detail his past actions. All the pain he had given to people he experienced himself, and all the pleasure he had given he received back again. But what distressed him most was that on this earth he had dormant in him a great capacity for understanding and that he had not used it. He could not get over it, and nothing I could say in extenuation served. "NO," he repeated again and again, "I ought to have understood, I had the capacity."

Certainly in his lifetime he had the faculty of living for the day only, and in a sense it is a most enviable one. Most of us cross bridges and ford streams so uselessly in our imaginations. But Jack knew unerringly where he had in his earth life so light-heartedly shirked the big issues of life. In his world, as he expressed it, "knowledge is." You don't wonder whether you know a thing or not. You know. Also, you don't forget. You are with people who are at the same stage of learning as yourself. As you acquire knowledge you pass on automatically into conditions embodying the results of apprehension. When Jesus Christ said, "In my Father's house are many mansions . . . I go to prepare a place for you," it is literally true. There are temples where people learn, and nothing is static. Conditions change in their world as rapidly as they do in this, so that no experience is ever repeated. When Christ returned

Listening In

after His incarnation, He founded a new temple of learning, so that the teaching He had sown as a small seed on our earth should be continued and expanded in the next stage of existence.

The fact that "knowledge is," makes argument non existent. When I said to Jack, "Isn't it very dull if everybody thinks alike?" it almost shocked him to realize how little of the joy of his life had penetrated into me. On the contrary, he insisted, it was most exhilarating - "more like living in Switzerland," and he was really distressed to think I could for one moment have thought it dull. I asked him if there was a sense of humour in his world and he said there was, only it operated differently. It isn't as unexpected as it is with us, for when they are with a person, they know his thoughts. That does not prevent him thinking humorously. They would say it in exactly the same way, and it would be just as much appreciated. With us a joke is generally a shock of delighted surprise - with them the element of the unknown is absent, but the joke *is* made and is appreciated - which is a great comfort.

Also they have a different standard of beauty. They keep the same form, but they never think whether a face is good-looking or not - it is just that person's face. There is a standard age. The old people go back and the young forward, so that all are, as it were, in their prime. Jack was very much interested in meeting an infant brother, who had only lived to be christened "Eric". He said one day to my complete surprise, as the baby had died when I was a tiny child, "I saw Eric the other day, I knew at once he was a brother, he is so like me."

He also made great friends with his maternal grandfather, who died long before Jack was born, but with whom he found a great many mutual interests, chiefly artistic ones.

It was at this time that he impressed on me most urgently not to think that his world was more important than mine. He had made the hitherto unknown most attractive and fascinating so that unconsciously I may have been living more in his atmosphere, and finding my own world a little difficult to concentrate on. He said there were degrees in matter and degrees in spirit, but no dividing line, and that I was not to think of my world as a material one and his as a spiritual one. Nothing is ever wasted, and it was vital I should realize the value of every action. "Nothing is wasted," he reiterated, and when I asked him whether it really mattered whether I learnt to play the piano decently, he emphatically assured me that all one does is ultimately used.

VII.

The subject of reincarnation is, I know, a controversial one, and repugnant to a great many people. Jack discussed it simply and accepted it unquestionably. He had never believed it when on earth, so I must pass on to you exactly what he said.

He was very excited one day, because he had been shown a vision, what his next life on earth was going to be, and he was thrilled. I was dismayed, for life here has never appealed to me very much. I had never had my brother's intense appreciation of it, rather have I always looked forward to the day when one can be free of the limitation of time and of space. So that when he came so full of his future life here, and I said to him, "Jack, you'll have to come alone next time, I've had enough," he said, "No, you are coming too." All my being rose in revolt, and I said, "No, never again." Quite calmly he answered, "Yes you are, but never mind now" — and then he explained to me the process.

Apparently we are entirely responsible for our lives here, and not that very much maligned power called 'providence'. There is no such thing as a square peg in a round hole. If we do not fit in with our surroundings, it is entirely our own doing, and we can and should only blame ourselves.

Before we incarnate, we are shown in a vision what our life on earth *can* be, and not till we return to the other world do we know how far

Listening In

short we have fallen of that possibility. But to achieve it *we must work*. There is free will in that world the same as there is in this. No one is compelled to learn. At universities here, a man can get a first, second or third degree, or even fail to pass; so, over there, if you idle your time away you incarnate badly equipped for the struggle of an earth life. Don't curse God for permitting the inequalities of life and happiness. We alone are the culprits.

Up to a certain point of development there is no choice. We have to go through a series of earth experiences until we reach a point when we can decide whether we can serve this world better by helping in it, or by influence on the other side.

One day, in a moment of despair, I implored Jack not to get too far on and leave me behind. I was haunted by a vision of an aged woman tottering across and finding the companion of years ago infinitely removed from reach.

"Olive," he said, "you don't know what love is when you say a thing like that." Then he added that all the energies of the next world are directed on to this one, because it is so far short, in its achievement, of what it should be. They work on the other side, not to get away from this world, but to *give* to it. It has got to be altered and improved, it has infinite capacity, and we have all - there and here - got to do our utmost for it. So if I, here, am working for the benefit of this earth, and Jack, on his side, is exerting all his energy for the same purpose - "how can there be any separation?" There is no distance between us but the *distance of our minds*. If I am writing this and thinking so vividly of Jack that I am persuaded we are writing it together, and I am suddenly interrupted and have to go to the kitchen and order the dinner, the only distance between us is this - my thought leaves him and is suddenly switched on to food and domestic items. "Sometimes," he said, "I'm nearer to you than if I was sitting on the sofa beside you." I knew what he meant. We all know the consolidating and also unfortunately, the dividing, power of thought.

VIII.

It is difficult for me to realize now how much I fully understood at the time and how long it has taken for the greater understanding to become part of my being. I cannot clearly visualize my state of mind before the conditions of the next world were made known to me, or what I should have been like if Jack's experiment had failed. There is as great a capacity in us all for scepticism and bitter rebellion as there is for understanding and love. Getting it clear in my own mind, I have lost all the reluctance I had when I started writing. In love it was given to me. In love I pass it on. Whether it is believed or not is immaterial. At least I have not prevented anyone from knowing.

There were other things that were possible to do, but that I could not achieve. I tried and failed. For one thing my brother always thought that I should see him. He tried so hard to bring that about. As I have said, I always felt him at my right side when he was talking through me; I closed my eyes and felt the power coming through the right side of my head.

One day when he was talking, I said suddenly, "Jack, where are you now?"

"Sitting in the chair opposite you," was the answer.

I looked, but could get no feeling of his presence there. Then he said, "Get up and look in the glass." There was a mirror hanging on the wall and I got up and stared into it.

"Can't you see me?" said Jack. "*I can see myself distinctly over your shoulder.*" I gazed and gazed, but could not see the faintest outline. All the same, he was confident then that I should do it one day.

He told me that when we think intently of a person who has passed over, we send them a picture, so that we can always keep in touch by cinematographing, as it were, on to them, all that happens. In the old days, I never bought a hat but wondered whether Jack would approve. To

Listening In

this day I "wireless" on to him everything I want him to know.

He went on to tell me that it takes us - as we know - nine months to get born, and three years to die. That is to say, when you first leave your physical body behind, you know, up to a point what laws govern the world you have just left, and it is quite easy to put those laws into action and keep in touch. But you have only a certain amount of energy to work with, and the strength of your physical vibrations - or rather the store of force at your disposal for "tuning up" and getting into touch with the physical world - diminishes each year, and I believe quite a different technique is needed after three years. For satisfactory results you must learn how to transmit, and you cannot do it single handed. You must have your receiving station, and the two must be in accord. Otherwise you get confusion and oscillation. Psychic people have a certain light around them - easily discerned on the other side, and therefore they may be used by all and sundry, much as a public telephone is used, unless they are careful. There are always numerous unemployed on the other side who have not adapted themselves to their altered conditions. They are invariably delighted to get in touch with anyone who will allow them to write or communicate through them.

When first I realized that I could write automatically I was pestered by a young woman who signed her name as "Hester". She never tired of telling me how she had fallen into the river one day, when she was picking forget-me-nots, and had most lamentably been drowned. I was terribly sorry for Hester when she first told me her tale, but grew exceedingly tired of hearing it over and over again. She had no tact. She would suddenly interrupt a most interesting communication, I would become aware that the handwriting had changed, and on asking who it was, Hester would reluctantly declare herself.

We can (sometimes) cope with bores in our world but we cannot deal with them on the other side. *Death alters nothing.* That is why this world is so terribly important. We must learn here. There is no one on the other side to force knowledge on us. We can continue to live by proxy in this world if we wish to. As the proverb has it, "You may take a horse to the water, *but —*." That same "but" operates right through the scheme of the universe. "Love is the fulfilling of the Law." If, when you pass over, you have loved and are loved, then there are always friends to help and show you the way, to point out the marvels and to admit you into the brotherhood of those like the Psalmist, who said, "Give me understanding that I may Live." Jack told me that the only suffering in this world is caused by lack of love. If anyone has shut himself in, a miser in emotions, or money, where self comes first and last, then there is suffering. If you can only get into touch with those you love, and you love no one but yourself. Laws are inexorable.

After I understood this, I got again in touch with Hester, and we had a long conversation about these things. I wanted her to realize that there were many wondrous things to think about and *do*, instead of eternally tumbling into the water and picking forget-me-nots. It is a little daunting to realize one can leave one's body behind and take one's bad habits with one.

IX.

At first, as I said, it is easy to get into touch. Later on it becomes more difficult and more complicated to get a physical connection. My conversations with my brother were very frequent the first year, almost daily, sometimes for a few minutes, at others for a whole morning. During the second year they were intermittent, and towards the end of that year, a month, or perhaps two, would elapse before he came again. Then finally he said he had only a certain amount of force which he could use to get into touch with our world, and he felt he could use it better to help us all by not concentrating on the talking any more. By that time the

Listening In

"rapport" between us was so close and so strong that I didn't mind. When alive we had found so often we could do without speech, and now I could feel his thoughts without the need of actual physical confirmation.

An interesting thing happened when I was staying away with a friend who had just lost her husband. We had been talking of these things and when I went to bed I had an excited feeling as if something were about to happen. I put out the light and lay down and then suddenly in the darkness I saw a series of pictures flash by, quite clear and coloured like a cinematograph, and my heart was racing and I could scarcely breathe. For I saw trees and houses and land, and I *knew* that the trees were not of the same substance as our trees, and though I knew I was looking at earth, yet I think now that it was of that new colour which Jack had told me of and which I can't describe - dark and radiant at the same time - houses - white houses, wonderful shapes - and they looked familiar and yet subconsciously I knew I had never seen houses like that before. They went so quickly and I truly nearly died that night of excitement for every moment I thought I was going to recognize "It," a feeling of strange expectation - and then they suddenly stopped. Whether physically I was incapable of receiving more I do not know.

The next morning Jack told me he had tried to send me pictures of his surroundings, but he didn't know whether I had got them or not. Nor have I ever known how accurate or how deficient was my receptive power to his interesting experiment.

For the first year we talked intimately of his and our affairs, for his interest in our lives was just as keen as ours was in his. He told us that in the life before his last earth life, he had lived to be an old, old man and we had all gone on and left him, so that it was quite fair he should go first this time!

We also discussed impersonal things. I asked him one day why it was thought necessary in Old Testament days to offer blood sacrifices to Jehovah. He told me that in those days it was necessary for impersonal sacrifices to prepare the way for the personal sacrifice embodied in the incarnation of Jesus Christ. There is a profound mystery in the act of the shedding of blood. The knowledge of the actual consistency of blood is a hidden mystery. He told me that Christ differed from every incarnated human being by the substance of His blood. In our world we use water to remove impurities. In a different sphere there is knowledge of the cleansing power of blood.

Also there is power in blood - the old magicians knew that full well. In absolute knowledge did Jesus Christ reveal the power released by the shedding of His blood.

"Greater things than these shall ye do, *because* I go to the Father."

Where are the great executive gifts that Christ possessed? *Within* His church today? Where is the prophecy? Where is the healing of the sick? Which of his ministers can perform miracles - discern spirits? Speak with tongues, cast out devils? Where is the real Communion of spirits?

Love, and not ecclesiastical formulae, is the link between this world and the next. I asked Jack whether he had come into direct contact with Christ and he answered "No," as he was not ready then. He made me realize that great events need as much preparation there, as important functions necessitate here. Life there is so human and delightful, logical and understandable, and the impression summed up in my mind by the word "radiant".

I asked Jack when he first started talking to me, "What about my head?" on account of the warning I had received not to do automatic writing. He told me not to worry. "I'll look after your brain." He certainly did. I never felt exhausted after our talks, on the contrary I felt vitalized. He undoubtedly passed into me much of his amazing individual energy.

It hasn't stopped there, but that is all I can pass on at the present. Our companionship continues. It was not a closing down when the faculty for physical contact became weaker. It has expanded slowly, surely, definitely. What the future holds for further revelation is not for me to indicate here.

Listening In

    I hesitated at first whether I should pass on to a certain member of my immediate family the fact of our daily talks. I dreaded at that time the natural inference that grief had unbalanced my usually normal mind. Jack emphatically urged me to do so. "He won't," he said, "be so surprised at coming over as I was." I did and I was astonished at the extraordinarily simple way he accepted the fact. Often afterwards he would ask me quite naturally whether I had heard from Jack. I also summoned up courage to tell one or two of his greatest friends. Though I was afraid that they might think me unbalanced, it did not seem fair to keep it to myself. I was rewarded, for I was given another proof (if I had needed it) of how entirely independent of me were Jack's actions.

    The friend with whom we had both been staying during my brother's last leave, came to Wooburn to spend the day with us. I cannot now remember the exact date, it was either late November or December, and I had resolved to tell him about Jack's communications. I knew he was not what the French call "croyant," and I did not really for a moment think that he would credit my story, but I didn't care whether he believed it or not, his great affection for my brother entitled him to hear it. He listened quite quietly and made no comment till the end, when he said, "When next you talk with Jack, ask him where he was this afternoon." The question utterly surprised me. I had been so intent on telling him, that I had not been conscious of Jack at all. If I had answered hastily, I would have said immediately that he must have been just behind me, on my right side, because I was always conscious of him there, it never occurred to me at that time that he could be anywhere else.

    The next time I talked to Jack, I said to him that I had told X all about it and he answered:

"Yes, I know, I was there."

"Where?" I asked.

"Nearly all the time," he said, "I was standing by the fireplace."

    This came as a great surprise to me, and I am ashamed to say I hesitated to pass it on to X. I did so want him to believe - and it was so outside my own conception of where Jack might have been. However, I soon realized that if I believed anything, I must believe everything, and so the next time I saw X, I told him that Jack had been in the room all that afternoon and that most of the time he had been leaning up against the mantlepiece.

X gave a visible start and said, "I saw him there while you were talking and I wanted the proof from him."

X is Scottish, and evidently has moments of Celtic vision, and Jack had been able to make use of that capacity to demonstrate to him his resurrection body.

X.

That is the note on which I wish to end this narrative, "RESURRECTION."

For two thousand years (with few exceptions), the teaching of the orthodox church has not dared to go beyond the climax of the cross. Yet if we study the life of Christ immediately after His crucifixion, we realize that His resurrection body corresponded in form to that of His earthly one. His disciples saw Him, conversed with Him, and ate with Him. His last commands, on which His Church is founded, were uttered on this earth after He had finished with His physical body.

Is it so strange, therefore, that those of us who love profoundly discover our capacity to follow in His footsteps along that narrow track, which through personal experience will in the future become the high road to knowledge?

THE TRAIL

LECTURES ON

THE TECHNIQUE OF REVELATION

By

OLIVE C.B. PIXLEY

Copyright
The Armour of Light Trust Council

As a sequel to her strange and vivid experiences in which she took part in ancient initiation ceremonies, the author describes how she was given the technique of revelation by which the power of light may be received. By a special training in which absolute consciousness and interpenetration of light is revealed, the initiate may attain complete spiritual contact. Showing how transmutation through light has been achieved at its highest by Jesus The Christ, the author communicates the knowledge through which this power may become again universally accessible with convincing truth and feeling.

THE TRAIL

LECTURES ON

THE TECHNIQUE OF REVELATION

By

OLIVE C.B. PIXLEY

With a Foreword by

LADY COBBE

Copyright
The Armour of Light Trust Council

First Published 1934
Revised Publication 1999

FOREWORD

The following series of lectures were delivered by Miss Olive Pixley and are an attempt to pass on to all who are interested the technique of revelation as she has received it.

In the first lecture, "Conscious Mediumship," Miss Pixley explains how this training started. She had then no knowledge of where it would lead her, and little thought that it was for anyone except herself and the friend, Madame Raoul-Duval, who has been the sole recorder. In 1931 I met Miss Pixley, was told about the technique, and began the training; since then many others have also come seeking it. The results have proved beyond all shadow of doubt that the technique in Light is a definite method, whereby all whose desire is great enough can train their latent capacity for contact with God; and through their trained awareness can themselves receive direct revelation.

I have been asked to write a foreword to these lectures, only because I can bear witness from my own experience that there is, in the world today, knowledge of the way by which someone with no special gift, no claim to merit, can scale those heights to spiritual certainty and contact with God which have hitherto appeared attainable only by the saint and mystic. A way which does not involve isolation and withdrawal, but which must be trod among the busy lives of men, for it is the way of living experience. A way which meets the urgent need of man here and now, leading from darkness into Light, from death into Life. It is the way of the Christian Initiate, leading inevitably to the esoteric teaching of Jesus the Christ.

I must attempt here to clarify certain points which arise in the lectures and which may possibly be obscure, since the lectures, with the exception of the first, were addressed to an audience who had already some understanding of this training.

To explain then, the use of the word "consciousness". We have learnt that close about us is the world of the invisible, the world of Light; not far-off heaven, but a world of actual substance, which not only surrounds us but should interpenetrate our whole being; should be that in which, with full knowledge of what we do, "we live and move and have our being." Life is a dual process, everything having its reality of happening in the world of the invisible, and its repercussion or tangible expression, in the world of matter. The cause of every event in the lives of men lies There; the effect only is seen here. Man, himself, has a dual existence; his soul, the light body of his spirit, functions in the world of Light; his human body, the material vehicle of his spirit, functions in the world of matter. Perfect balance would involve a perfect conscious co-operation between all three - spirit, soul and body. Because of his ignorance and blindness man separates the functions of these three, insulating, as it were, the world of matter from the world of Light, his body from his soul; and, as a maimed creature, amputated in half his being, moves in a world of friction and disharmony. Yet there lies in every man, inherent but dormant, a capacity for awareness of spiritual things; a capacity for spiritual consciousness, which, trained and developed, can fuse him into wholeness, making him able to function in harmony with both worlds.

To a dawning consciousness comes the knowledge that where there is lack of harmony in the human personality the cause must be sought in the man's untransmuted spirit. Sin is a condition of man's spirit when it is separated from God; a spiritual disease which manifests itself in the flesh by those acts of violence and disharmony which men call sin. There is also a condition of man's spirit when it is in perfect harmony with God. We have learnt that when Christ told his friends, "I go to prepare a place for you, that where I am there ye may be also," He was speaking of veritable fact. The consciousness of Christ is the place of harmony which He has prepared for men. Not a realm only of the hereafter, but an actual living reality for the incarnate spirit of man. A condition into which the man who has developed his consciousness can and does enter and abide; in which the spirit of man makes his contact with the spirit of God, and by that contact finds himself transmuted: spirit, soul and body. It is from the consciousness of Christ that conscious man draw not only the food for his soul, but the power and strength, the inspiration and direction, the very

Foreword

essence of life, which all men need so sorely to readjust the balance of their lives and the lives of all the nations of the world today.

Consciousness in man is, therefore, the capacity of the individual to enter into, absorb, and be absorbed by, the consciousness of Christ.

The technique in Light has been given to us by revelation, and we, who have followed the steps of this training, have proved by experience that it is a means whereby the unconsciousness of the individual, the cause of all friction, disharmony and sin, is transmuted into consciousness, and the individual capacity is ever increased. We have learnt that, for the modern world, this training is the Christian Initiation, which is the process of "becoming" sons of God. St. John records that "to as many as received Him (the Christ), to them gave He power to become the sons of God." The first step in the Christian Initiation. St. Paul describes the perfected Initiate: "as many as are *led* by the spirit of God, these are the sons of God." Between these, Alpha and Omega, lies the whole gamut of the experience of "becoming".

We do not paint a way of roses. The scaling of great heights is always an arduous task, and often the feet of the mountaineer are cut and bleeding; yet this we know, that when a man has found the "pearl of great price" he will not rest content until he possesses it. The conscious soul may suffer greatly as it passes through the stages of self-revelation and transmutation; yet these are but the pruning process, leading to the full fruiting of the Tree of Life, and cannot compare to the barrenness and desolation of the world-agony, the results of unconsciousness.

A final word with reference to the technique. It must be understood that this is no formula which can be handed out from the lecture platform to cure all ills. There is nothing secret or mysterious about it, but it is a process of training, each step leading inevitably to the next. To desire with all one's being to see the infinite panorama from the mountain heights, and to breathe the pure mountain air, is not enough; the actual process of climbing the mountain must be undertaken to reach the fulfilment of the desire. We can only bear witness to our certain knowledge of the path to the infinite wonder those mountain heights reveal; to the urgency there is for all men to leave the valleys and claim their rightful heritage. We can only cry with a loud voice that all may hear, "This is *the way*, walk ye in it."

WINIFRED A. COBBE

CONTENTS

	Page
Foreword	35
Conscious Mediumship	41
The Worship of Light	54
The Freedom of Two Worlds	64
Revelation. The Revealing Power of Light	74
The Law of Transmutation	86
"All I Have to Give"	97

CONSCIOUS MEDIUMSHIP

Lecture given February, 1930

It is essential to discover the sharing point - the common denominator, as it were - of all spiritual research work, from the individual point of view; and it seems to me to be summed up in the word "consciousness," the "awareness" and understanding of what is happening to us. It is also important to have clear in one's mind what one considers the normal, the sub-normal and the super-normal.

The perfectly normal person is the one who is as sensitive to receive spiritual as he is to receive physical vibrations.

The super-normal are those who are more psychic than sane.

The sub-normal are those who are merely sane, and have no knowledge, as yet, of their spiritual side.

We all have the capacity for psychic development, and it is as much a part of our spiritual selves as our hands are of our physical bodies. We can use our hands as Kreisler does, or Rodin did; or we can break dishes, or pick oakum. It is always the same instrument.

We have the capacity for consciousness, but we are not naturally conscious beings. We do not know; we wonder; we theorise; we disagree; and often we do not care. Sometimes I feel that we have suffered, not for Eve having eaten of the fruit of the Tree of Knowledge, but that she took such a ridiculously small bite.

Thus, granted our capacity, the next thing is the technique. I want, as shortly as possible to tell you how the knowledge of that technique was given; how, step by step, it was slowly revealed to me that it is possible to get in touch with one's full consciousness.

At first I thought it was impossible to pass on, in any detail, the process. But I am aware of such an urge on the 'other side' to find normal people capable of receiving and recording the knowledge, that this effort to make public a private experience may be of value and help those who are travelling along the same road - looking for a signpost.

The Trail

Those of you who have read *Listening In* will remember that outward intercourse with my brother ceased in the third year after his death, except on very rare occasions and at long intervals. For several years afterwards I can recall nothing of psychic interest. I may have, occasionally, psychometrised various objects; and then, without any warning whatever (and I must admit, without any conscious desire on my part) the work started.

Looking back on these last five years, I can see so clearly now the marvellous staff work on the 'other side'. Sometimes I had the feeling that it was in the nature of an experiment with them, and they were faced with a great many difficulties. When I talk of 'they' and 'them' you will know that I am referring to the delightful individuals on the 'other side,' who have been so infinitely patient, and so extraordinarily clever, in the method by which they conveyed to my mind the facts concerning the two spheres.

One of the first things they had to do was to find a recorder, and special qualifications were needed for that job. Infinite patience, a trained artist, an accurate mind, and perfect friendship. These they found in Madame Raoul-Duval. We met in September 1924. The following spring I went to stay with her in her farmhouse in the hills behind Cannes, surrounded by olive trees and vineyards; and there, out of the blue, the work started.

I am going to take you straight from the starting-point. Two normal people, out in the south of France to enjoy themselves. I had not written, then, the little book. Psychic phenomena were not in either of our minds at all.

A great many years ago Madame R.-D. had lost a friend, and, knowing my psychic gifts, asked if I would try and get a message through. Ever since my brother had used my head I had never tried automatic writing, as I disliked that form of communication, for I could not guarantee the individuality of the controller of the pencil; and I refused.

One day, however, when we were sitting under the olives, having coffee after lunch, I happened to have my writing-block near me. The sun

Conscious Mediumship

was shining, I was smoking a cigarette - it was all so sane, so normal. A sudden impulse made me turn to her and say: "I don't mind trying now," and, taking up block and pencil, I waited. Suddenly the pencil started drawing a curious little picture that conveyed nothing to me - little hillocks with telegraph-poles at odd angles, disappearing into the distance. That was all. I passed it over to Madame R.-D., saying: "This is for you, but I think it must be nonsense." But she recognized it at once. Years before she had gone to Algeria with this friend, and there, one day, out in the desert, her friend had said, laughing: "Isn't it absurd to come right out to the Sahara and see all those drunken-looking telegraph-posts!"

More convincing than any message was that little drawing of an incident known to only two people and overheard by none.

Directly after breakfast the next day I tried again, and to my astonishment I was made to put down book and pencil. I got up slowly and unhesitatingly started gestures and postures, Egyptian in character, in that I never walked with my feet side by side, as we do, but toe to heel, and all arm movements with stiff wrists, outstretched hands and fingers rigid and close together. I have never been to the East; but from what I have seen of Egyptian bas-reliefs and drawings I thought it was due to the craftsman's perspective that one always sees Egyptians portrayed walking lengthways. I found it just as easy and quite as quick to walk this way. I never made a mistake, nor hesitated, and I had to take positions which are extremely difficult for a Westerner to take.

When I started, Madame R.-D. tried to draw the various positions that I was assuming; but she too was included in it, and I, knowing unerringly the double movements, went with her through the various ceremonies. I did them with my eyes shut; but my inner sight was so clear that I could walk from one end of the room to the other, put Madame R.-D. in the position she had to be in, never fumbling to find her hand, never touching a piece of furniture, and using the different things in the room for the proper setting. Often I had to arrange the room beforehand: take things from different parts of the house, never knowing to what use I should put them; but in due course were absorbed in the harmony of the ceremony.

This occupied the early part of our mornings; and every day I went through a different ceremony. For six weeks I never repeated a single one.

In the afternoons I drew a free-hand design, drawing lines across the page which unexpectedly formed a definite design. What was real drudgery was that I had to go through, in single gestures, the morning's ceremony, picking out a definite line in the drawing that represented the gesture I had just made, and marking it with a strange sign. Thus we had the ceremony in the morning, the shape of it in the afternoon, and a language; none of which we understand.

When we returned to Paris we were made to read Budge's *Book of the Dead*, and found we had gone through the ceremony of the "Opening of the Mouth," and much more of the ritual concerning the eyes and the ears than is contained in that book.

We had worked for six weeks. And it ended on Whit-Sunday of 1925. I returned to England, bringing the books of drawings and hieroglyphics with me, hoping to find someone who could tell me what strange language I had been transmitting. Instead of help I got plenty of good advice to give up dangerous practices. One eminent Egyptologist told me that "some of the signs were undoubtedly Egyptian in character, though none were pure hieroglyphics." I went to the British Museum and found traces of Sanskrit, Sumerian, etc., and was helped to the conclusion by a scientist interested in occultism, that I had probably got down Atlantean characters, from which all languages have sprung. There I left it.

Soon a conviction came to me that I had to make arrangements to work during the coming year at stated intervals; Advent and Lent particularly. As the work had to be recorded, and as we both lived in different countries, and as I was not a free agent, either domestically or economically, I thought it was going to be exceedingly difficult to arrange. One cannot say: "I feel I am going to have a psychic experience in November!" It fact, it was the sort of work one could not talk about.

Conscious Mediumship

However, it was arranged perfectly. And then we went through the Hermetic mysteries.

I had to get plasticine and wax, and model forms and animals that are not on the earth today. These were used in the ceremonies. We were made to read Meade's *Thrice Greatest Hermes*, of which I am ashamed to say I was completely ignorant. I enjoyed modelling those strange things; and it was difficult for Madame R.-D. to have to watch me - she, who was longing to use her gifts. In those days, when we were just starting, it was very hard for her merely to record. But we both realised that 'they' could only use my ignorance. Her technical knowledge might prevent her from doing the thing 'they' wanted in 'their' way. She would have wanted to have done her best in *her* way. For instance, when I realised that the plasticine was developing into a camel she longed to take it from me and make a proper camel out of it. But I had to give it a strange head-dress, with curiously designed trappings, minutely marked out with the aid of a hairpin, and distort it from the anatomical point of view.

Every evening I modelled the necessary forms for the next morning's work.

Strange things, also, I had to do with light and reflections and shadows. On one occasion I had to put three electric lamps on the ground, at certain distances, so that they cast my shadow on the wall three times, and at three different heights. Then I had to do certain gestures with the arms, and Madame R.-D. had to stand a few paces away and do the same, so that twelve arms and six heads were moving simultaneously. It gave me the most extraordinary feeling to see those rhythmic shadows and to know it was only we two in the room. For I had, first of all, to brush our hair straight up from our foreheads and the back of our heads, into a cone shape; and to see those Buddha-like heads on the wall, and to know they were really our own, was an experience I shall never forget. One seemed to have a threefold consciousness - our material selves of the twentieth century; our Eastern shadows; and the mystic understanding of what we were bringing into our consciousness.

Then there followed a piece of work which interested me more than anything I had yet done. It was concrete. We excavated a temple at Petra, and at the same time we went through the initiation of the neophyte and learnt the secrets of the priests. It is not possible to give details of any particular part of the work. I only want to record how it happened and the actual net result. When I say 'excavated' I must try and describe the means that were employed. Daylight was essential, preferably the strongest sunlight; and secondly perfect quietness. Then my mind seemed emptied of all transitory thoughts, and slowly an idea developed, just like the developing of a negative, until it stood out clear and detailed, and I could see and feel it with my mind.

The temple dated from a very early period in the history of Petra, and it was dedicated to the knowledge of the Rose (at least, what I have been forced to express as 'The Rose'); the symbol was a circle faintly indented in four places. The roof was marvellously carved inside with this symbol; and outside, rather high up, it occurred again. I got the feeling that this temple was small and very secret, but the source of true knowledge. No blood was ever shed there. The service was entirely voluntary, and the priests had a wonderful understanding of the inner life, of which life here is the symbol, and the mystic life the reality.

In the excavating of the temple I started by being the mason, sculptor, painter, and a host of different craftsmen, who had all helped to build and beautify it. I was, in turn, priest and neophyte. I paced certain dimensions, so many paces north, south, east and west.

It is extraordinarily difficult, when one is experiencing a super-normal sensation, to find words vivid and vital enough adequately to express it. To give you one example: I knew suddenly one morning that I was out-of-doors somewhere in the East, and I started pawing and scratching the carpet of the room where I was working; and I said, laughing, to Madame R.-D.: "I feel exactly like a hen scratching the ground, only I am out in the sun and my feet are bare, and the sand is very hot." I felt the sand covering my foot, and then I knew it had touched the top of a stone urn - which I excavated and held up. I felt the shape of it and knew it had a dome-shaped cover to it which I took off, and saw inside a dark, sticky substance, made of rather revolting things mixed with serpent's blood. And then I knew that it was used by the priests for certain rituals (which I got about three weeks later), but it was not kept in the temple, as it contained unclean ingredients; so was buried in the sand outside and only used occasionally.

All the time one seemed to have a super-consciousness, not letting go of one's sense of humour or one's critical faculty, or one's ordinary senses of sight and hearing. I would hear the telephone bell ring in the distance, and yet be aware of the sensations of the neophyte undergoing certain mystic ceremonies. I can only compare it to listening in to a B.B.C. programme, and being aware at the same time of sounds from a different station, both quite different, and neither cutting the other out.

How enjoyable those weeks were! I was as thrilled every morning as any archaeologist could possibly be. I never knew whether I would get a description of the various inner temples which were kept for different degrees of worshippers; designs of the statues, or the revelation of priestly secrets. And it was only at the end that I was told that the temple had existed at Petra.

I also got a description of an ark, and the indication of where it now lies buried. That, too, was enthralling. I found that the two figures on either side of it were made of gold, pounded with precious stones - not stones inset, but crushed into splinters and mixed with gold. And I have never yet been able to find words to give a really accurate impression of its perfectly beautiful design and craftsmanship.

And then from that work which I loved, I was made to go on quite different lines, which I frankly disliked. The glamour of the past was still on me, and I was taken, most reluctantly, into the future. I had to design an aeroplane which would be driven - not by petrol - but by the contact of a ray of light of inexhaustible energy, which as yet had no focusing power on the earth. I called it the 'magenta ray,' as that was the nearest description of the colour that I could get. Not being a mechanic, and hating machinery, my heart was not in this work. But it had to be done.

The Trail

I approached two scientists after it was finished, as I wanted to pass it on. One could not touch it, as he was in Government service, and his time was not his own. He said he thought I was a hundred years ahead of my time; but added that if he had seen a wireless apparatus forty years ago he could not have touched it either; and he is now a great wireless expert. The other man was interested when I showed it to him, but suffered from a reaction afterwards to the thought that knowledge of any worth could come through psychic channels.

The temple at Petra had ended my work on bygone civilizations; the 'magenta ray' started my work on abstract propositions; these were followed by an intensely interesting six weeks in the spring of 1927.

Before we left Paris for the south I knew we had to buy some modelling clay for Madame R.-D. to use: a small quantity, but I did not know for what it was wanted. Down into the glorious sunshine we went, and Madame R.-D. was told to model a head, rather smaller than life-size, and two hollowed-out sections of the same head, divided down the middle. The clay that we took down was exactly enough for the purpose.

Every day I was instructed in the functioning power of the brain, for ultimate healing purposes: exactly what part of the brain controlled the bones, blood, nerves and emotional processes. We were given the technique of healing, but both of us were perfectly aware that we had not yet the power to use the knowledge.

Then followed instructions for developing our individual consciousness, and I was made aware of what I can only call 'The Christian Initiation.' I realised that Christ was conscious man: that He knew, scientifically, how to apply the laws of this world to the service of mankind. His miracles were not haphazard evidences of a sporadic power, but a scientific application of His knowledge. He *knew* what He was doing. I was convinced that understanding and controlling the elements, walking on water, disappearing into space, transmuting His physical atoms in three days, were examples - not of His divinity - but of His perfect manhood: the highest expression of life in matter that the world had ever seen. It was the perfect equilibrium of earth (magical) and

Conscious Mediumship

spiritual forces.

I was made to understand, without a fragment of doubt in my own mind, that to reach the ultimate understanding and fulfilment of life one must follow the Christ line of teaching. The old philosophers will take one far, the magic circle will take one deeper and farther, but the Christ was the spiral - height, depth and interpenetration; that was the truth I had to apprehend before I was ready for further instruction.

In the spring of 1928 I definitely started on the conscious development, i.e. getting in touch with one's conscious body. The human body is not a conscious entity. We know nothing instinctively of its intricate works; we depend on doctors for special information about our own property.

The first step towards making a contact with our consciousness is through breathing. Conscious breathing is exactly the opposite to physical breathing. It is up and down (instead of in and out) starting from the solar plexus. When it was first revealed to me, I thought: "They want me to do an up and down breath in one breath, and I can't." But by degrees I understood. Those of you who have read *Listening In* will remember that my brother found conditions in the next sphere completely reversed, that what was inside here was outside there, and vice versa. I had not fully understood at the time, but now it was made clear. Our bodies, over there, are composed of particles of Light, instead of dust, as our flesh is here. Light is as concrete in a world composed of different conditions of Light as matter is concrete in a physical world.

In our light bodies there are no internal organs. Breath goes up and down instead of in and out. I had to 'think' my breath from my solar plexus to my feet, and straight up to the invisible point of a triangle, the base of which rested on each palm of my hand. The intake of breath had to be thought down to my feet, the expulsion forced up. We were given exercises until conscious breathing became as easy as ordinary breathing, and we immediately felt certain results.

Then we were taught something about sound. Sound is the creative force. "In the beginning was the Word, and the Word was with

God, and the Word was God." Now, the Word is a sound, and just as a good musician can, through the medium of his instrument, transmit melodious sounds, but does not create them, so we, through the medium of matter, can transmit God, but cannot create Him.

It is recorded that the walls of Jericho were shattered by the agency of sound. A glass can be broken by the sounding of its particular note. I venture to suggest that the Pyramids may have been put into position by sound. You can create and destroy; you can remove mountains by faith and knowledge. In the old civilizations they knew the power of sound; and the future ones will know it again. Never again for magical and personal power, but in love and service for the whole of humanity.

And then with sound and breath came colour - a vital force. In the next sphere, amongst its many activities and properties it includes travelling. Here, if we want to go to any particular destination, we have to find out which station provides a train to take us there. In the next world we have to find out which *colour* will take us where we want to go. To make a contact with this earth we must take the trouble to find out on which line of colour to experiment. It does not come instinctively; we have to learn.

Colour has its opposite - as light has darkness. There is a neutral quality attending colour, an interval between keeping colours inviolably intact. This opposite is also a condition of creation, a constructive medium - elastic, supple, colourless - a material from which form is shaped by thought. We use bricks or concrete or wood to build a house. The fundamental material for construction in the next world is this supple medium - the complement of colour.

Colour is that element of the conscious body which corresponds to the blood in physical man. At the same time, colour is outside man as earth is outside him, although his physical body is made up of earth.

In this world, two halves make a whole. In the next, two opposites make a whole. In matter you cannot square the circle; in Light you can. Once, in a vivid blue light, I saw - for one disintegrating second-

Conscious Mediumship

a sapphire circle perfectly squared. And I wasted many sheets of paper trying to transmit it.

All that I heard of colour was outside the radius of time. I was taught nothing of its rate of vibration, but a greater understanding of its functioning powers. It is by the knowledge of the interpenetrating power of colour, sound and breath, that the conscious and physical bodies become one, and we KNOW. And your knowledge no man taketh from you.

Conscious mediumship is a very gradual process, and it depends entirely on the individual what progress is made. No definite results are promised. It is an act of faith, and it is at times as difficult to believe that definite results will follow as Naaman found it hard to credit that by washing himself in the Jordan seven times he would be cured of a loathsome disease. He was prepared for an expensive and sensational cure.

In all psychic work one does definitely hope for the sensational result - the event which will prove, once and for all, to the sceptic that such things are true. But consciousness does not function along sensational lines. It must be the personal experience that provides the individual conviction.

The only thing that conscious knowledge costs is the effort to acquire it. Often the transmitter may be in the next sphere and the receiver here. We have, in this world, to get sponsors for admission into clubs or societies; and people who will lend their names and use their influence in getting jobs of material value for their friends; and there is as much detail and organisation for peace and harmony on the 'other side' as there is for commerce and prosperity here. If the necessary conditions are not fulfilled then the results are unsatisfactory.

To those of you who wish to develop your 'awareness,' do not say to yourself: "I am not psychic - it is no good for me." By that attitude of mind you are completely cutting off any possibility of communication. It can never be forced on anyone. If you want it enough, it is there. If you hold yourself 'aware', you are bound to receive some impression - though probably not an obvious one.

From the beginning I was taken by surprise. None of us have identically the same lives from the material point of view, and none of us will have identically the same conscious development. Do not give up all your time to it. Develop every gift that you have on the human side; artistic, business, literature, agriculture, whatever it may be. Your spiritual development must add to the fulness of life and must never detract from it. But do not try to take any short cut through a third person; that is utterly useless; there is no value in it, unless it comes direct into your own conscious understanding. And record everything, even if you think it is quite trivial.

One must be physically fit - harmony right through one's being. If one is nervous, run down, definitely ill, one can make little headway. The body must be fit, the head clear, the nerves relaxed. It is like any wireless instrument: if the battery is run down the sounds cannot come through.

The conditions that I find ideal for working in are: daylight and quiet; in the hot sunshine - the humming of bees, and the many earth sounds. The most wonderful things have come through under those conditions. Although it seems that none are really essential; for I have worked in every sort of room, in many different houses. It is not the material conditions that matter, but the spiritual. It is the condition of one's mind that is important; the taking and stretching of the mind, till comprehension makes a contact and the knowledge can pass through. That, to me, is the essential difference between trance and conscious mediumship. In trance you allow your physical body to be used by spirit entities making a material contact; in conscious mediumship the mind is developed to a degree of sensitiveness that it can make a contact with spirit entities in their own sphere. The difference between host and guest.

It is not a physical condition, it is a spiritual experience. In itself it is absolutely safe. No one on the 'other side' who was not working for the highest development of the human consciousness could take you along that particular line. You are taught, quite dramatically, to recognise the

Conscious Mediumship

right from the wrong impulse. Twice I was tempted to obey an impulse which made it possible for me to produce a rather exciting magical effect. The second time I lost consciousness and felt very ill. The third time I stopped instantly, recognizing the difference between the spiritual and the material; and though I was tested at intervals, I always knew. That occurred when I was doing the old ceremonies; and I was very grateful for the severity of the test. For, of course, I should have been of no use if I could not distinguish between the real and the false.

That is the danger of trance mediumship: when you allow yourself to relinquish and someone else to make use of your consciousness you can have no guarantee of who is going to make use of you.

I am not sentimental about the conditions of the 'next' world: I am intensely interested in them; but, for all of us, it is this world that matters. It is our 'job' to understand the marvellous powers lying dormant in humanity.

All that I have been taught is for the purpose of making us better citizens here, for raising the level of the human race - the development of the soul and the body. To do that I had to start at the very beginning; and I consciously went through the mystic ceremonies of the earliest civilizations, right on to the Christian Initiation, and the transmuting principle of life.

Of all the great initiates, HE is the only one who demonstrated to an incredulous world that there is no death.

He transmuted His body and He consciously knew how to do it. The facts have survived two thousand years. The faith has been kept alive. The knowledge has scarcely yet been tapped.

THE WORSHIP OF LIGHT

Lecture given on January 26th, 1933

All the knowledge that I have accumulated of the worship of exterior Light I have received through the psychometrising of stones standing on ancient sites, such as Avebury, Stonehenge and stone circles on Dartmoor and in different parts of Devonshire. Other strange worships I have come across in Brittany and Yorkshire; but I want, this evening, to concentrate on the worship of the sun, the moon and the stars.

It all started by my handling a tiny little stone figure, put into my hands by a friend with whom I was lunching. This friend has travelled all over the world, in the remote places of the earth, and she told me that this tiny figure had been given to her by an archaeologist in Mexico who had told her that he knew it to be so old as to be ageless from the historical point of view. She gave it to me to hold, asking if I could get anything out of it.

I held it, and almost at once I was in a vast underground cave, not dark, but with an iridescent metallic light coming from the walls. The cave was light as daylight, but the emanation from the walls was of a totally different substance of light from any kind that I knew, so I called it metallic light. Then I saw that there were people and that they had large square heads, and were very short of stature. Their eyes seemed to give out light, in the same way that a dog's or cat's eyes shine in the dark. Then, quite suddenly, I knew that the sun was their devil. They were terrified of the power of the sun. If exposed to its rays they would die. The only time they ever went above the ground was when the moon was visible. The moon was terrible, but she was also beneficent. The sun was evil incarnate and meant instant destruction.

I was so enthralled in what I saw that I look back on that little figure as my first real travelling companion. My body has never been outside Europe in this incarnation, but my mind has been taken on the most wonderful journeys.

The Worship of Light

It was the result of that trip to Mexico that brought me into contact with a friend of the owner, who was so intensely interested in archaeology and had a special theory of his own of the alignment of ancient sites. He hoped that I might be of assistance in substantiating his theory. Wonderful, indeed, is the working of destiny. Hot on the trail of his own theories, he took me to these ancient sites, accompanied by the owner of the little figure; took me to the very places that I had to go to, where, hidden in these fragments of ageless stone, lay the records of man's contact with God.

On our first expedition we went to Stonehenge and Avebury. Every impression that I got through has been fully recorded. Avebury belongs to a very ancient civilization. I refuse to postulate any periods as Atlantean, or pre- or post-Atlantean. I only know things as they are, not where they occur in the division of allotted periods of time.

The race of people who built Avebury did not build it on any constructional plan known to us within that period of time we call history. It came through me that they built - in those days - stone replicas of living objects, and Avebury was constructed in the form of a serpent. The entrances were guarded by two rearing snake-heads, and I knew that the curve of the body of the snake formed the circles of the inner temples. I sensed that it was a very holy place. All that has happened since the destruction by time, and circumstance has not defiled that first pure worship of Light - the trinity of the heavens, the Father sun, the Mother moon, and their starry offspring. I have been to many places where that sense of defilement and desecration is very strong, but I have been to no place where that sense of pure holiness is as strong, as vital, as I most unexpectedly found it to be at Avebury.

Then came Stonehenge. The fundamental basis of the worship there was the sun, and a definite placating of the moon. The strength and purity of the worship at Avebury was their knowledge of the force and harmony of Light. This was marred, as it seemed to me, by the Stonehenge fear of the moon. They seemed ignorant, there, of the law that governs the impingement on matter of the rays of the moon. Ignorance is the parent of fear. They concentrated on the force of the sun. They also understood acoustics in a way that modern science has not yet touched again.

There was a certain stone there, and, when I put my hands on it I was immediately in a niche, almost a small room, alone, with a great semi-circular stone corridor on each side of me, and I knew that exactly opposite me at the end of one semi-circle, and the beginning of another, was the high priest, or oracle. I knew that I was the voice of the people, and that, on a curved breath, I sent through the stone passage the request, and the answer was sent back to me along the opposite curve. The sound was no louder than a sigh.

And then another stone that I touched gave me a knowledge of the science of balance. Perfect proportions can be perfectly balanced. I got a system of dovetailing great blocks of stone for the roof, each resting in perfect symmetry on the other. There have been a great many theories as to the original construction of Stonehenge. To me it seems quite outside the capacities of architects or archaeologists to speculate on that construction until we know why it was necessary to build it at all. They did not erect building in those days for the protection of the race against the elements, as men do now; houses to keep out the wind, rain, and cold; and for our animals, stables and farm buildings. In those days, aeons before the Christian era, they built to co-operate with the elements. They not only worshipped the Light, but they knew how to draw the rays of the sun into their very being. They did not just worship with their minds. Their ritual included the knowledge of how to draw into their bodies the creative energy of the sun force.

I came across the same thing in Devonshire, at a place called Drewsteington, the remains of one of the most wonderful centres of initiation in the West. So little of it is left, but that little is alive, a vital record of a wonderful past race who lived, loved and learnt the mysteries of life with an energy and passionate vitality of which I can give you only the faintest idea. Their religion was not remote, the worship of a glowing disc, so far from the earth, so inaccessible to humanity. They knew their

The Worship of Light

God. They became part of Him.

Those of you who know Dartmoor know well the multitude of stone circles scattered all over the moor. I was taken to one that gave me the key. It had never remotely entered my mind before that there could be any scheme of construction that united them. Here I got a picture of a little stone temple in the shape of a star - a special star - and the temple would only be used when that star was at its zenith. It was not used just to worship its brightness, but was a little storing house of stellar force.

It came through to me so strongly that the heavenly bodies, the planets, the various constellations, and even the comets, were reproduced in stone on Dartmoor, Salisbury Plain, and possibly other open places where I have not been. Today there is a general idea, but very scanty knowledge, of stellar influences at birth. We all know that horoscopes are occasionally very accurately cast. The influence of individual stars on physical conditions was a science in those days, a divine mystery into which priests were initiated. The place of initiation in the West was Drewsteignton; a vast, a marvellous university, where the mysteries of the laws of life were taught and lived.

There was a co-ordination of sound signals and worship all over the moors and plains. I tapped one receiving station, but it was a cold, wet day, and it seemed so complicated that I did not go fully into it. There was something missing; but the sound seemed to come in on a spiral, and go hissing up in a rocket-shaped sound. I think that the shapes that sounds make on the air were known and exploited in the Stone Age.

The knowledge of stone was an exact science. There is a vast stone circle in a huge field at a place called Stanton Drew, where I was taken, hoping that I might substantiate a theory formed as to the original construction of the place.

With my eyes shut I quite clearly and in detail saw a vast stone building, far larger and higher than Olympia, but of oval shape and domed roof. At one end was a raised part, and on it was a huge block of stone. I knew it was the interior of a great masonic university. On the raised part stood the Master-mason, demonstrating to the apprentices below the basic principles of stonecraft. At the other end of the hall was another huge block of stone, and there were a number of men striking it with stone implements. The Master-mason was directing their blows as a conductor controls an orchestra. With every ringing blow on the lower block I saw the one on the platform quiver and move, until it moved into the required position. And then I knew that the Master-mason was a scientist in stone. He knew the substance of it, the laws that governed it, those of attraction and those of repulsion.

I realised that vast blocks were as easy to move as the smaller ones were; that it did not depend on muscle or on machinery, but on the natural law of sound, which, when understood by man, can move material mountains and control the elements.

These ancient people lived on a co-operative basis with the laws of their world. Of the intervening stages, when, little by little, the exact science got carelessly handled, inaccurately passed on; when, to get the needed result spurious methods were introduced; of that period I know nothing.

In all the work that I have done I have only been able (or allowed) to pick up the basic principle of construction. These ancient people were true scientists, and true worshippers of Light. I got a feeling that their's was an universal knowledge, and that when I go East I shall pick up again that knowledge of oneness, that sharing of substance, that man had - in those days - with his Creator.

Today, all over the world, we approach God on wavelengths of sound. We pray with words, the reiteration of words, but we have not yet the universal knowledge of how to make ourselves one in unity of substance with God, who is Light, Light of Light, the essence of Light, the absence of all darkness. In darkness lurks fear, ignorance, bondage.

Fascinating as it was to tap these ancient mysteries, there was in my mind no longing to return or to dwell on them; or to utilize again those formulae for increased physical vigour. For, at the same time, I was being taught the reality of the power of that Light which can function in one's spirit.

The Worship of Light

Man is composed of two irreconcilable substances - spirit and matter. I was being taught through psychometry that the law of life which governs the material world is the action of Light on matter. If the rays of the sun and of the moon and of the stars had had no focusing point in this world; if there had been no substance to attract Light, then there would have been no life as we know it on this planet, at all.

In the same way I was being made to understand that the life of the spirit is Light, the food of the spirit is Light, that all revelation comes through the agency of inner Light - not as a symbol, for it is as much a reality as the action of the infra-red rays; that the law of Light, working through the spirit of man, sets in motion the law of transmutation.

It was the knowledge of the working of this law that Jesus the Christ, incarnated to give to the world. He lived it, demonstrated it, fulfilled it. He did not just talk about it; He was the Law made flesh; Light incarnate in matter.

Every day, now, in the newspapers we read of some scientific revelation of the power of Light, and of its infinite capacities. What our generation owes to exterior light - to gas, to electric light, the elimination of darkness - is hard, perhaps, for us fully to appreciate. We take it so much for granted, until, by some accident, we are deprived of its use. I suppose that it is equally impossible to estimate the spiritual darkness of the world until the Christ came, to give every individual the knowledge of how to make a direct contact with the divine source of Light, the Father. He Himself knew how to make that contact; knew how to make Himself a focusing point. He was able to demonstrate the infinite power of Light operating through the human mind. He put into action the law of transmutation, He changed the substance of man's flesh, in the flash of a second, from a condition of disease to that of perfect health; He changed the substance of water into that of wine; He controlled the elements.

I have been taught that the 'next' world is composed of compressed Light - at least, that is the nearest description that I can give of it. Our bodies over there are also a composition of Light. Colour is a fundamental principle of Light; therefore, it is a radiant place in which to find oneself.

Light is the common denominator of these two worlds. Matter belongs to this world alone, and has no power in itself to change its condition. Light can transmute matter, changing its substance. In matter lies the process of decay, in Light there is no decay. Exterior light works in conjunction with heat. Inner and spiritual Light has no heat; it works independently of the body; its direct action is on the mind.

One's mind should control one's body. Therefore, if one's mind can make a conscious contact with divine Light, and if one learns how to make one's spirit a focusing point, then we, through our hands, our mouths, our whole beings, can demonstrate again the law of transmutation, as it was done two thousand years ago, and as it was promised it should be done again even with greater power and force. The facilities for understanding the power of Light are infinitely greater in these days than they were when He gave His teaching to the twelve.

To gain knowledge of Light must ever be a voluntary accomplishment. There are two methods of teaching - one, by fear, compulsion; and one by love, attraction. Knowledge of Light eliminates fear. It is the only process by which one can transmute fear into fearlessness; doubt into certainty; faith into knowledge; and strife into peace. This is not rhetoric - it is real: as real as the light is in a room.

I was told how it could become real for me, and for all human beings who want that reality for themselves. Inner Light can only make a conscious contact with the human mind. It is the exact opposite of the functions of the body, which are mostly unconscious. We feed our bodies, and are quite unaware (most of us) of the properties, creative or destructive, of the nourishment we give them. We take what we like the taste of; and reject, when we can, the things we dislike; that is the basic principle of adult consumption of food.

We cannot unconsciously make a contact with Light, nor can we confuse it with any other human sensation. We cannot control it. It is stronger than any degree of human imagination; and when we are learning about it, it is always outside the scope of our comprehension. It

The Worship of Light

is the power that enlarges our vision; develops our capacities; dissolves our limitations.

Light is the substance of our spirit as flesh is the substance of our bodies. If we desire to acquire perfect equilibrium, we must know how to feed our spirits. On the enlightenment of the mind depends the health of the body. The reconciling of the opposite elements in man - spirit and flesh - is accomplished through the agency of Light, through this law of the transmutation of substance. The substance of our egoism is pride, greed, hate, self-will, indifference, frustration, bitterness, every attribute of decay.

All the love in the world cannot change the substance of our spirits in spite of ourselves. Love can show us the way; it can prove it can be done, but it cannot do it for us. That is why the knowledge of conscious development cannot be forced on anyone. The method by which we can develop our conscious understanding, so that our spirits can make a direct contact through Love and Light with all spirits who dwell in the world of Light, cannot be printed and published, and given to all and sundry; but it must and can be given to all who desire it.

For there is a method by which we may obtain the secret bread of life; this knowledge, not only of praying to our God, but of knowing how to draw His substance into our beings, that our spirits shall be as much a part of His spirit as our bodies are part of our parents; part of His very substance, sons of God, children of Light.

The power to make a contact with that ancient worship of Light, this gift of psychometry is one result of the conscious training. Quite possibly is was a dormant quality, but one that would never have had a vital existence if my mind had not been consciously developed. Light can only make contact with Light. Once that contact is made, a gradual process is started; all the dormant qualities are slowly stirred, and one becomes conscious of capacities of which, hitherto, one had been completely unaware. And so it continues until, the training accomplished, the power of manifestation should reveal itself, not in any predetermined way, but according to our capacity.

The Trail

To make a contact with Light, one has to start visualising it; the whole process is the gradual expanding of our powers of visualisation. You cannot imagine it if it is not there. Sometimes a vision is flashed on to the mind, and one begins to see with the inner eye. Something that has been puzzling is suddenly made clear; and so the teaching in Light starts. It is not just a thinking way; it is also a living way. It must come first. It must be one's whole desire, the pearl of great price, if one wants not only to worship, but to *be*, the Light.

I would like to pass on to you a vision that I had not so very long ago. It happened on one dreary afternoon in early winter. It was in London, and it was raining. I turned away from the window and the room seemed quite dark. I shut my eyes, and suddenly I saw a great ray of Light shining down from infinity on to two worlds - the one on my right higher, and on a different level from the one on my left. The higher one seemed to be a globe of pure incandescent light, and I saw it was absorbing all the strands that came from the great blinding white ray, and it was of a pale golden colour.

Then I looked at the other world, which I saw was quite dark; and yet the white ray was blazing down on it, with the same strength. And I saw on top and rising from this world was a soft, dark, impalpable substance, through which the Light could not penetrate. Then, as I continued to look, I saw a comet of Light flash from the ray, cleave right through the blanket of fog, and reach the earth. I *knew* that it was the Christ, the master of Light, detaching Himself from the ray of purest white Light, the quality of which I have no words to express, penetrating through this substance which resisted the ray. I also knew that the darkness of the world had nothing to do with the lack of exterior light, the sun; but lack of this white, heatless Light, so vivid, so brilliant, that one's shut eyes flinched away from it.

And then as I continued to look, I saw tiny little lights spring up on the earth quite far apart, and tiny trickles of light run along the ground, joining light to light; and then I saw that these lights had minute thin filaments that penetrated through the dark vapour, and were merged in the

The Worship of Light

the great ray. And I saw that the dark blanket was not fog lying on top of the world, as I had supposed; but an impalpable substance, rising from the earth and coming out of the heads of the people in the world, accumulating and forming this substance that resisted the ray.

I think I was rather stunned when that vision faded; when the full import of this world's possibilities dawned on me, and I realised that it could only be achieved by individual effort.

In my youth I had longed to die young, to be rid of these frightening limitations of time and space; and of my sense of utter frustration. Now I am just beginning to live; to realise that it is in our humanity that we must find the key to life; that, until we find it here, we must of necessity return again, and again, and again. Think of this world when every single soul in it consciously knows whence he came and whither he is going; when he realises that he is the entire master of his fate; that there is no circumstance of life that his spirit, co-operating with the law of Light, cannot transcend.

Darkness, evil, fear, hallucination is only the absence of Light. Where Light is they have no power whatsoever.

Light makes no contact with darkness, or darkness with Light. Therefore, if the Light is in you, you need fear no evil; it cannot touch you. Evil makes a ready contact with unconsciousness; it can always take a person unawares. Where there is fear you may be sure there is always a darkness of mind. Where there is Light there can be no fear.

It is only possible to give the merest outline of the experiences of these last years; what I have left out would fill a volume. It has been like putting together a very intricate jig-saw puzzle. Tiny fragments were handed to me, and I had to put them on one side, because their shape did not fit in with anything that had been given me before. Slowly the pieces accumulated, and there was nothing that I could do about it, for I knew that the pieces were alive, and that they were growing together; but even then I did not know whether there was a real picture, or just a jumble of pieces; until these last few months, when the outline was suddenly made clear to me, and I knew that it was a key.

THE FREEDOM OF TWO WORLDS

Lecture given on Ascension Day, May 25th, 1933

The key that I mentioned in my last lecture ensures for us the freedom of two worlds - this material, human world, and the world of Light, the spiritual world.

We must, as complete individuals, understand once and for all, that it is as necessary for us to comprehend the laws that govern the spiritual world (those laws which our spirits either obey or disobey), as it is essential that we should investigate the working of natural laws that affect our physical body and material conditions.

The laws that govern matter, and the laws that govern spirit or Light are not at variance, but are in complete harmony, and interpenetration. In our ignorance, in past ages, spirit and matter have been thought irreconcilable substances. In our knowledge of today we have re-found the law that unites all apparently irreconcilable conditions; and that is - the Law of Transmutation.

The understanding of the working of this law gives us the freedom of knowledge - power on earth - the power that defeats death.

Our knowledge, or lack of it, is our individual responsibility; the parable of the talents is a very searching one. Knowledge can free us from the karmic law; ignorance that binds us on earth, binds us in heaven; knowledge that frees us on earth, frees us in heaven. Therefore it is essential that we obtain our freedom here. So essential is it, that we must endeavour to eliminate all prejudice and all pre-conceived ideas, and examine unemotionally the source from which this law, which can transmute the substance of matter into the substance of Light, originated.

Knowledge of that law was given to the world, through the incarnation of the spirit of the Christ, into the human personality of the conscious medium, Jesus. Every human individual is controlled by a spirit, and the spirit receives its individual name in infancy. We do not name the body, we name the spirit. A still-born child has a perfect

The Freedom of Two Worlds

human body of flesh, blood, bones, nerves and brain; but it has no breath, no life, no spirit; and it receives no name, no individual sound.

If we begin to examine the statements of the New Testament regarding the activities of Christ, we come across the most amazing facts concerning His power to demonstrate the working of this Law of Transmutation.

We find that He was able to recall from the world of Light the spirit of Lazarus. In the immediate functioning of the Law of Light, this re-animation of matter, He was able to demonstrate this new law to a people who had been instructed by the Scribes and Pharisees concerning the mysteries of the past civilizations. Those mysteries had not included a knowledge of the co-ordination of the Laws of Light and the laws of material substance. He proved to them that the requisite amount of Light, incarnate in the proper proportion of matter, instantly makes a corpse into a perfectly healthy human individual. I say 'individual', for it was not only the re-animation of a body; He restored the spirit of Lazarus into his own healthy physical body, by the instantaneous fusing of laws.

We cannot understand any branch of science by instinct; we must be taught, and we must be willing to learn. To master the intricacies of physical science needs great mental application and concentration, coupled with an urgency to learn; and that is a straight and narrow path of service. To develop the capacities of one's mind, so that it is possible to comprehend the infinite expanding transcendencies of spiritual science needs also mental concentration, united to an earnest desire to acquire knowledge, and treading with unfaltering footsteps the scientific path of service.

I have just said that every human body is controlled by a spirit that we know by its baptismal name. The quality of that spirit is manifested by its actions, and what we call its characteristics. From the social point of view we roughly divide human nature into two classes - the controlled and the uncontrolled. In the former class the proportion of Light and matter are well balanced; in the latter, matter pre-dominates, and offends against the law of proportion.

We all know the difference between the qualities of exterior light; candle-light, gas, electric light and spot-lights of intolerable brilliance. I want you to realise that the substance of incarnate spirit varies as much in quality as does exterior light. The spirit sustains and increases its quality according to the strength of the source that it draws on. If the spirit is unaware of, or repudiates the existence of spiritual energy, it must of necessity, deteriorate. If the spirit is of a slovenly nature, and not at particular as to where it derives its nourishment, and changes its diet according to its mood, it will suffer from as many spiritual discomforts and diseases as the body does, if it follows the same regime. That is why Christ claimed His divinity, because He knew that He drew into His being sustenance for His spirit from the true source of Light. No power on earth can separate the substance of the mother from her child, and no power in Light could separate the spirit of the Christ from the spirit of God. So - given the unity of eternal substance - what is the effect on the human individual?

I see the personality of the man Jesus as the perfect conscious medium, controlled by the spirit of God; and that, I claim, is what we all should be: conscious mediums controlled by the omnipotent spirit of Light.

It was as a medium that Jesus consciously transmitted the knowledge of the divine laws to the world. Never did He claim power of His own. He knew what He was doing, but He knew that the knowledge was the result of direct inspiration, which could only make a contact with His mind, if He deliberately transmuted the grosser qualities of His human substance into the incandescent essence of spiritual energy. That took Him thirty years to do. Then He became God's medium. He spoke with the voice of divine authority. Through Him the Creator was able to control the elements; through Him, not *by* Him. Through Him the power to transmit sufficient Light into the spirit of man, to re-adjust the predominating balance of matter, so that the diseased body became whole, was manifested. Through Him the knowledge of Light was established as a scientific accomplishment.

The Freedom of Two Worlds

Through the ages there have been individuals who have had mediumistic qualities; of that we have legendary and historical evidence; namely, the oracles, magicians, witches, mystics and the twentieth-century medium: all making some contact with super-normal conditions, and all testifying to various experiences outside the range of the normal individual.

Psychic experiences were quite usual in the New Testament days. It was very difficult for the people to discern the source from which the individual drew his power. If the results appeared the same, did it matter - said they - whether the source was Beelzebub or God?

Does it matter whether our experiences are psychic or spiritual? Does it matter whether our knowledge comes from the astral plane - the plane of hallucination - or from the world of Light, the plane of reality? There lies our individual responsibility; we alone know where our desire for knowledge rests.

There is in most of us a great craving for illusion; something that will take our minds away on a holiday from the grim realities of our everyday life. Everybody has some power of imagination, some secret place of phantasy, where our spirit relaxes and withdraws from the immediate present. It may consist in dreams about the future, castles in Spain, or those gossamer veils that drape our minds when we return incognito into the past, and wander at will in those pleasant realms of unreality.

Our minds have the power to create the conditions that our souls demand to live in. If our bodies are hungry they demand to be fed; if tired, to rest. If our souls are tormented by the restrictions of their incarnate conditions, if their creative power is thwarted, if their craving for beauty is denied; then, in ignorance of the power of our spirits to transmute the restrictions and limitations of our material environment, they create for themselves the necessary illusionary conditions to ease the pain of their torment.

Will you look on your mind as the builder and architect, your spirit the material, and your soul as the owner and occupier, all these working in such close co-operation that it is difficult to separate them? What I want to emphasise is that your soul is bound by the restrictions placed on it and around it by the qualities of your spirit, and the constructive or destructive energy of your mind.

If your spirit, working in harmony with your body, through the agency of your mind, creates for yourself, in this world, an atmosphere of harmony, dealing with the realities of life at their true and not their fictitious value, you are, through the medium of your mind and spirit, creating for your soul your heaven on earth. But, if circumstances are too strong for the mind to cope with, if the spirit is weak, if it creates for itself synthetic conditions, if it does not know from where to draw its strength, it continues with increasing energy to draw its force from the world of illusion, the astral plane.

Look for a moment on the astral plane as the theatre-world of the mind, where it can legitimately create for the soul pleasant - or unpleasant - conditions, according to the quality of the spirit that controls it. There are many illusive conditions in this material world that deceive the physical eye; many startling optical illusions. On the astral plane there are as many and varied conditions calculated to deceive the mental vision. In this world we can 'fake' new furniture to look genuinely antique; on the astral plane the mind can create synthetic conditions of beauty that will deceive the uninitiated into thinking, temporarily, that they have reached the home of eternal realities. But they find that on the astral plane there are all conditions of minds. The depraved, the sadistic, the ruthless minds can also create the conditions for which their spirits provide the material, and in that condition their soul must live, until the spirit changes its quality, and understands that the Law of Transmutation is the key that unlocks the door to freedom.

The soul is the individual note in the eternal harmony of life; the spirit is the tone, the quality, the expression of that note; and the mind is the instrument that plays it. The inadequacy and inefficiency of the instrument is responsible for the appalling discords that provide the destructive energy that is so evident in the world today. No change, either

The Freedom of Two Worlds

for construction or destruction, can take place in this world, or on the astral plane, except through the agency of man's mind. Therefore, the whole future of the world's welfare lies in the minds of men living today. It lies, individually, with us.

The whole responsibility was shouldered, primarily, by the soul of the Christ. Could He, in full knowledge of that responsibility, incarnate in matter, learn the technique of drawing the necessary quantity of the essence of Light into His spirit, as daily food? Could He transmute an ordinary, normal, Jewish mind into a delicate instrument, that could express, in utter perfection of tone, one perfect note, the standard pitch to which all humanity could tune in?

He did change the condition of minds that made a contact with His own mind; He made men understand that mind and spirit can dominate all substance, even that intangible condition of hallucination. If only people could realise that reality can be far more beautiful than phantasy, that there are legitimate retreats where the spirit can travel to and rest, and bring to the mind fascinating material for constructing a radiant environment for the soul.

The spirit has a two-fold activity; the power of drawing in, and the power of radiation. It can draw into the mind any form of illusion, and through the mind can express any form of unreality. We all know people whom we cannot trust, who often appear to believe genuinely in the truth of their own fantastic imaginations. There are some people who prefer to live in a world of their own, of make-believe, with themselves very much as the central figure. We call them megalomaniacs, but they are quite happy in thinking themselves all that their fancy paints them. Where - when their spirits leave their bodies - can their minds go? Only where their spirits can lead the way - to their favourite haunts of illusion on the astral plane. There are many people today who think that because a spirit has passed out of the limitations of the physical conditions, the mind automatically become receptive to eternal truth. They believe that any information that comes through from a spirit on the astral plane, must have more value because of its discarnate conditions. If the spirit is of the substance of unreality, it must, of necessity, make a contact with its own kind; and if truth is demanded by the sitter in this world, and truth cannot be discerned amidst all the unreality that surrounds the control, then the *appearance* of truth is all that is available.

Unreality is only intolerable to the spirit that yearns for reality, and - as I have said so often before - Love is the force that makes the spirit aware of its potentialities. There is no limit to the power of Love; it can change the spiritual condition of all souls, incarnate and discarnate. Love sets in motion the Law of Transmutation of matter into Light. Every spirit has the same basic composition as its Creator; therefore, every spirit has fundamentally the same capacity for development. Its capacity for Love can be stimulated into far greater activity by the contact of the love force of another spirit. The Law of Love makes instantaneous response inevitable. Therefore, if we know how to radiate this power of love into the spirits on the astral plane, to make them aware of reality, we can direct their minds towards the realities of the world of Light. We can, in the flesh, give to those who want it, the key of freedom. Love is never helpless. Ignorance makes us slaves.

Will you visualise, for one moment, the radiant world of Light; then, visualise this physical world as you know it. Then, picture the connecting corridor - the world of phantasy and illusion - and try to visualise what happens to your spirit in sleep. Your spirit will go, in sleep, to its habitual rendezvous, wherever that may be. If it is in the realms of detective fiction, it will revel in the thrills provided by the minds that can produce, on the astral plane, living replicas of the printed word. These replicas have no creative force behind them; they cannot actually do the things they appear to be doing; they have no force of their own. They are the creatures of the mind, puppets of phantasy, terrifying or entrancing according to the type of mind that has produced them.

If the natural flight of our spirit in sleep wings its way to the realms of reality, the world of Light, we can pass through the corridor of hallucination so swiftly, so surely, that no impression of unreality is retained by the waking brain. We wake with a sense of refreshment, and

The Freedom of Two Worlds

often with a great reluctance to start another day in this inferior world. It depends on the state of our spirit, before we go to sleep, whether we have a straight trip through or have what we call a broken night. We all know those short, unsatisfactory glimpses of unreal conditions, the pursuit and flight from malignant or grotesque forms; that wandering down eternal corridors; packing, or trying to, and never reaching any destination. Such conditions are tormenting for a spirit longing for that all-pervading sense of balm that comes from contact with even the suburbs of the city of reality.

The mind does not function on the physical plane, in sleep. It is never divided in this life from the spirit. The spirit leaves sufficient light in the body to keep it alive. The mind works the whole time; and, according to the material provided by the spirit, it builds the environment for the soul. It builds by night, it builds by day, this mind of ours. Freemasons we are, all of us; and the great architect of the universe is our Master Mason.

When you go to bed, to ensure freedom of transit in sleep, from this world to the world of Light, pray for protection on all planes; and in addition, visualise yourself as a cross of Light, from the top of your head to your feet, and acrossways over your heart. Hold it in your mind, and have no fear. The protection of Light is a reality, and no power of darkness can come near.

What the Christ set Himself to do was to make a path of Light, straight from the world of Light, through the astral plane, to the earth; so that spirits should be able to travel in freedom from this world to the next, immune from the power of darkness. What all conscious spirits are trying to do is to make that path into a thoroughfare. That is what they are doing, our loved ones on the other side; widening the road, sending us the material for our spirits to do our share of it. They cannot do it all themselves, being no longer in the flesh, but they can show us how they are working, and get us to co-operate. That is the note that our spirits must tune up to; that our minds must work to produce. Co-operation. If only we can become delicate intruments through whom He can work;

conscious mediums controlled by the spirit of God.

The knowledge of the freedom of our two worlds lies in the achievement of the Ascension. If the Christ had been unable to construct the pathway of Light from this world back to the world of Light, then, indeed, would this world have remained the cul-de-sac that our ignorance often imagines it to be. Step by step He retraced His way back. He knew the scientific formula. He prophesied the results beforehand. He realised the effect it would have on the minds of the people. He knew it would take years in time, for the knowledge to penetrate into the the minds of men. He knew it could only be accomplished through the power of Love, essence of divine Light. Unless He accomplished His return, there would be no pathway for the great spirit of Light, whose individual note, or name, is TRUTH, to make any contact with the spirits of His initiated apostles, whom He left to carry on His work. The coming of that spirit of Light would *prove* to them that He had accomplished the return journey. The blazing of *the trail* had been achieved. His work was finished.

Can we begin to realise what that work was? It was not only defining a hitherto unknown law, it was fulfilling it. The Law was made flesh. The descent of His spirit into matter was the incarnation; the conscious return of His spirit was the ascension. The Christ's is the only spirit that has ever achieved a conscious return. "Be of good cheer," He said, "I have overcome the world." Like all scientists who serve humanity, He left the formula behind to be used by those who came after Him. Whose fault is it that it has been locked up, and the key mislaid? Not for us to enquire, not for us to judge. Past failure is no excuse for present inertia. The knowledge He gave to the world is our rightful inheritance. It was a world gift, this freedom of intercourse between His world and ours; this uniting of knowledge between incarnate and discarnate minds; this illumining of a pathway through the world of illusion, straight to the gateway of reality. He *was* THE LIGHT OF THE WORLD, and there was no other way of return to the infinite Light except the way He took, by transmuting the substance of His flesh into the substance of His spirit. It was accomplished by the energy of His mind, generated by the power of Love, and, through that power, He was able to build for His soul, His eternal habitation.

That is the key that liberates every imprisoned spirit, that transmutes the insulating conditions of men's minds into the vital power of transmission. It has been ignored, misunderstood, abused, rejected, scorned. It is the key that will unlock all mysteries, reveal all hidden knowledge; that tiny little key, made of the pure gold of the essence of infinite Light that is called - LOVE.

THE REVEALING POWER OF LIGHT

Lecture given October 19th, 1933

The urge to talk about the revealing power of Light came in June of this year (1933). The experience that life has provided in the last four months has crystallized for me the form that revelation can take in each individual life. It is the goal that we all should endeavour to reach. It should be the apex of our ambition.

When men or women go to the university they have to pass a qualifying examination before they are able to become members of that university. If they are below the standard, they are unable to enter in and become part of the academic life. Those who do join the university have at stated times to pass various examinations as tests of their capacity to learn, and finally qualify for their degree. There are definite privileges in the universities of all countries available to those individuals who pass their examinations for the highest honours, and are hall-marked, as it were, for all their earthly life as possessors of first-class brains, worthy of the highest distinction which the world of learning can bestow. All the world recognises the value of first-class brains in science, economics, art, literature and music; in many cases we consider these individuals to have been inspired - the work they do is far above the normal capacity of the average man. This evening I want, if I can, to make clear the difference between the power of inspiration as an active force in life, and the power of revelation; for they are two completely different conditions.

In my last lecture I tried to clarify the different functions of the mind, the spirit, and the soul; if I had not attempted this, I could not hope to make clear to you the difference between inspiration and revelation. Our brains can be inspired - but only through the sanctification of our spirits can our souls receive the wine of revelation.

The soul is our eternal ego. Spirit is the eternal life-principle that animates the human body, and is that activity of the soul that corresponds, in Light, to the circulation of the blood. The brain is that sensitive

Revelation. The Revealing Power of Light

material instrument which, vitalised by the spirit, becomes the mind, thus uniting the finite and infinite principles in man. Once the soul has incarnated, it becomes subject to the finite laws; it is a hostage, as it were, in this finite world; it is the captive of the mind of man. While it is incarcerated in the body the mind of man is the dominating factor. He can control his spirit. He can surround it with the walls of prejudice, fanaticism, fear or avarice; he can reduce it to a negligible non-entity, while his body obeys with moderation, or breaks with excess, the laws of nature. And his body will thrive or suffer accordingly.

But the mind of man has no authority over his spirit in sleep, or at death. In those two conditions his body has no dominating control; his soul is the centre of his spirit's activity. On earth the average man is supremely unconscious of, and indifferent to, the existence of his soul. As a means of expression his body appears to him to be an adequate instrument; he can express, through his different members, every note on the octave of emotion, from the gentleness of love, to the violence of hate. The soul is the radiant ego of Light, which, being of the same substance as God, makes us all divine. It is the work of the spirit to try and print indelibly on the mind of man the image of his own soul.

Inspiration is a condition of power, the power of manifestation. Very often it is not a conscious condition at all. An orator may be inspired to make statements that will avert a crisis, that have surprised himself as much as his hearers, at the unexpectedness of their delivery. In moments of acute danger a man may be inspired to perform an act that will save many lives from destruction. An artist may paint a picture that will inspire men's minds with a sudden understanding of infinite beauty. A poet may capture an immortal fragrance, and in rhythm and sound hold it captive in print. But that condition of inspiration, that fleeting and elusive quality of power does not change the character of the man's mind. It has no quality of transmutation; it does not make your orator a moral man, it gives him no power to live as he speaks. The man who saves many lives, may not know how to save his own. The artist whose work is an inspiration, may live a life of degradation, and the poet may utterly fail to make love a fragrant reality.

No man doubts the capacity of all these individuals to make a certain contact with immortal power, but it is obvious that it is not a stable condition of their lives. Theirs are the minds that make an unconscious contact with, to them, an unknown source of power that lifts the level of their self-expression from average to the brilliant heights of genius. They may, individually, have no conscious knowledge of the working of divine power; they may even repudiate the existence of a divine creator; they may even arrogate to themselves that flame of creative energy that urges them to express, as perfectly as human capacity allows, the vision that illuminates their mind with the brilliance of a possible achievement. But no genius can invoke the power of inspiration unless his spirit knows the right-of-way. We want to discover that right-of-way, which will enable us to make a constant and instant contact with that quality of divine power that stimulates the mind, enlarges the vision, and makes life a radiant whole. In the case of an inspired genius, the spirit is able, in brilliant flashes, to introduce that man to his creative ego, but it is not able to effect a union between the two. That must be a voluntary, conscious act; the deliberate abdication of the power of the mind to the controlling force of the spirit, the domination of the soul, and the subjugation of the body.

If man knew for certain the extent of his own possessions, this internal strife for domination would cease. If he could know himself and become aware of his divine capacities; if he could become aware of the co-operative conditions that exist, he would know that outlawry is always doomed to failure.

You may think it unimportant, or too difficult, to try to visualise these different activities of our individual egos, but I cannot sufficiently stress the importance of trying to do so. Every medical student has to learn the intricacies of the mechanism of the body and brain. The soul is the replica, in Light, of the material body, and the spirit is the active principle of both. In perfect man the soul is, as it were, the lining of the body, the inner substance of the chalice that contains the wine. When the

Revelation. The Revealing Power of Light

body dies there is no barrier between the union of the spirit and the soul. As long as the body is alive the spirit struggles to effect this union, and can, as I have said, with sensitive minds, make men aware of their potential greatness.

Life here, in this world, is the quest of the spirit of man to find and possess his own soul - the Holy grail, the chalice of Light. That is all that reincarnation means; this returning again and again, until we can, in perfect consciousness, merge our finite with our infinite selves. That it has been done once, we know. The soul, the spirit and the body of Christ were one living radiant force. When He achieved that, which He did at the age of thirty, He was able to lay the foundation stone of a new temple, not built with hands, but constructed by the power of the spirit working through the human brain, a receiving station, as it were, for the revelation of divine truth. He spent the next three years demonstrating the results, which He maintained must inevitably follow once the contact with the Father was achieved. His heart ached to see all the suffering around Him. He longed to give this knowledge to the whole world, but He was under no delusion. He knew the minds of men better than they knew themselves. He knew that all the suffering and agony in life was caused by ignorance; He knew that He had the capacity to love the whole world enough to teach them, but there were so few who could love Him enough to learn. I wish I could in any way give you an adequate understanding of the steps by which my own certainty has been achieved. It is the pilgrim's way - but it does lead to the gate of revelation.

I started by referring to the various examinations necessary to achieve academic distinction. The body is really only a replica of the soul, or light body, and our spirits go through as varied a set of tests for the soul's progress as it does for the human personality. The spirit passes on and up, in spirals, and every fresh spiral provides a new set of experiences. It needs the most tremendous effort of will and transmuting of our spirits to achieve a new spiral, and it can only be accomplished by preserving our mental equilibrium. The force that can preserve our human poise under great spiritual stress is Light; not that condition of light that plays on our human tissues, but that ray which illuminates our minds, down which every form of inspiration flashes and which brings to Light all hidden things of darkness.

Remember, the spirit and the soul are composed of Light; the body and the brain of matter. The spirit, working through the brain, creates the mind, and the mind registers the activities and quality of the spirit; therefore, there is always the minimum of Light in every man, and the maximum was achieved - as I have just said by the spirit of Christ.

The method by which man can increase the strength and activity of his spirit is the developing of his conscious understanding; the deliberate taking off from his eyes the blinkers of illusion, and the facing up to the fact that, to possess his own soul he must lose his egotism. After all, one's egotism is only one's unconsciousness, and not much loss, but one of the most difficult of all achievements. The first step towards this union of body and soul is accomplished through learning to breathe consciously. Breath is a rhythm. All the functions of the body - breathing, sleeping, waking, talking, eating etc. - are automatic gestures. We do not think before we do any of those things; we do not consciously digest our food.

In the developing of our awareness we cannot make a single automatic gesture; we must consciously know and record the twitching, as it were, of every conscious nerve. The teaching in Light is for the developing of one's visualising powers, for it is only through the vision that the spirit can increase the capacity of our mental understanding. In learning to breathe consciously I want to stress the fact that it requires no physical effort. It is no yoga system that imposes a strain on the lungs, and by virtue of a physical effort produces super-normal conditions of the mind. On the contrary, the body has to be so relaxed, so utterly at ease, that in visualising the conscious breath you become aware of your spiritual potentialities. The next step is the drawing in of Light; and the visualising of this brilliant ribbon of intense whiteness is not a matter of imagination, as all of us who are faithfully treading along this pilgrim's way can testify. Light *is* - and no strength of the most fervent

Revelation. The Revealing Power of Light

can make the Light come, or make it do what we want; for Light teaches us and reveals the way to us. I can pass on to you, as it was given to me, the technique by which you can all achieve your individual experiences. Failure to achieve those experiences lies not in the Light but in us. There are as variable conditions in Light as there are different substances in matter; different qualities, different activities, different rhythms, myriads of colours, and one by one, and step by step, the spirit reveals to conscious man the inexpressible radiance of the world of Light.

Like the undergraduate, however, we have consciously to pass our tests before we are qualified to make a contact with the more powerful conditions of Light. I begin to understand the Beatitude which says: "Blessed are the poor in spirit, for theirs is the kingdom of heaven." The rich in spirit, with their accumulation of intellectual discoveries, their facility for acquiring many languages, so that old mysteries may be studied, rare documents deciphered, find the interests of their brains so absorbing, the Epicurean feast so satisfying, that the spirit gets little chance for revelation. What allure can a draught of pure spring water have for the man who possesses a vintage cellar? To the master of dialectics the inflexibility of the Law of Light is sheer antagonism. He cannot match his blade with the sword of the spirit of truth. So the law of reincarnation provides the necessary experience for man, until he at last realises that no intellectual achievements, no accumulation of the knowledge of other men's minds, draws him nearer to the divine essence of his own being. Only the emptying of himself, the voluntary renunciation of all inherited prejudices, and even loyalties, by the withdrawal from his mind of all protective barriers, can he, at long last be open to the revealing power of the Light.

Revelation is the sharing of a divine secret, the rending aside of the veil of the temple. It is having, as it were, the ear of God. That is why I said at the beginning that it should be the apex of our ambition, for we hold within ourselves the possibility of achieving it. It is not prophecy - for there have always been false prophets; but revelation in Light can never be untrue, for truth is of God, and God is Light of Light.

There are infallible tests wherewith to distinguish gold from the baser metals; and the infallible test for prophecy, divination, manifestation and revelation is whether its source is from the world of Light.

I have said that the quest of man in this world is to fuse his finite being with his infinite self. The quest of the soul in the Light world is the reunion with, but not absorption by, the unit of brilliance whom we call God.

The texture of the incandescent radiance is the very essence of Love, and every soul is a fragment of that eternal substance. The oneness, yet apartness, of that soul is as individual as that of a newborn child, who is a fragment of the maternal substance. The home-coming of the soul - child to its divine parent - is an odyssey written in the world of Light by the Christ Himself as a guide for the children of Light. Here, we have the New Testament, which tells how a man can find his infinite self. St. John gives the whole secret away. Those of you who have the leisure and the interest, will you re-discover for yourselves how often Light is mentioned in the New Testament, and in what connection? Those of you who are doing the Light exercises, and those who are not, do try and see what significance you can extract from these references. Take them one by one, and visualise the scenes as clearly as you can, and see what differences in Light the various instances provide. It is most illuminating.

I have often wondered how much those early painters knew, who depicted Christ and His apostles, and the saints, with haloes of Light round their head. In reading the Revelation of St. John one is struck with the difficulty that he had to find adequate words to describe the wonders that were revealed to him. "Like unto an emerald," he says, "a sardine stone," "gold," "crystal," and all those jewels that reflect light and the glory of colour and brilliance. Again, his attempt to describe those unknown living creatures: "Like unto a calf, a flying eagle . . . full of eyes round about and within." He was struggling to describe that unknown world, that world of Light that you and I can enter, and know for ourselves his difficulties; and know, also, how near the truth he was.

Revelation. The Revealing Power of Light

I often think that the Church has looked upon St. John as the first and the last word in Revelation. He was, indeed, faithful to the limit of his capacity; which capacity is within the reach of all souls whose spirits have linked themselves in perfect unity with their human personality. The failure of Christians has lain chiefly in the fact that they have tried to imitate the actions of Christ, and have mistaken 'doing' for 'being'. If only they had understood the method which enabled Him to 'do' because He 'was,' if only they had understood when He said: "I am the Light of the world, no man cometh unto the Father save by me." There was the right-of-way revealed to them. God was Light; He, Jesus, was the Light of the world; therefore He was divine. It was a fact, not a boast. It was so simple, so utterly obvious, if only they could understand. There was not a single thing that He did in Light that they could not do; they were of the same substance as Himself, soul and body, Light and matter. If only they could learn from Him how to make this contact in Light, then these marvellous things that He did, they could do too, and even more marvellous. It was for them, and it is for us, to continue the experience, and to test for ourselves the certainty of His method.

The greatest antagonists to Light, I feel, must always be the orthodox minds, for Light is so unorthodox, so unexpected. "The wind bloweth where it listeth," but there is very little freedom in orthodoxy, founded, as it was, on the laws of the Old Testament: "Thou shalt not." Christ said: "Thou shalt love."

No one can put a boundary round what we shall do; but a very high fence indeed can be erected by those in authority who have the right to say: "Thou shalt not." There is no human authority in Light; no high places; no boundaries; no limitations; no inferiority complexes; no pride; but there is knowledge; wisdom; inspiration; manifestation and a radiance of the soul, through the human personality.

There are many minds who think that faith is the only necessary qualification of the spirit, and that the absence of faith indicates a non-spiritual nature. There are also numbers of people who simply cannot believe in the paradoxes of the Christian religion. Faith is a necessary

necessary ingredient of the spirit; one must believe a thing is possible to be able to make a start at all; but to stop short at believing is to sterilize faith. Knowledge must, of necessity supersede faith, and that is where orthodoxy has been completely culpable. There would be no schisms in the Churches; there would be no failure in Christianity; there would be no wars in Christian lands; no revolutions; no suicides; if they had only obeyed the one direct command He gave the world - "Thou shalt love." If only they had not stopped short at believing it to be possible, but had done it. Faith without works is dead. Do not just believe in the working of Light, do not think that it is only possible for some people, do not be afraid that it needs a psychic qualification, or necessarily a good brain. Light is a divine force; your spirit has the same capacity as every other spirit to make a contact, and a direct contact, with the spirit of Christ; and just as much as when He was alive, He insisted on making a personal contact with the youngest child, with social outcasts, and with men like Nicodemus - a master in Israel - so, now, there is no question of qualification, except in desire. If you want it you can have it; that is all.

In the whole training of Light it is only a question of desire. That is why the rich-in-spirit find it hard to believe that so simple a way can lead to so great a goal.

Along the Light of Revelation, comes the executive quality of Light. The training is the developing of the power of our minds to visualise the Light, and - step by step - our capacity increases. By drawing in the Light we feed our spirit; and, as our spiritual strength increases, slowly or quickly our infinite self, our soul or light body is revealed. But this fusion of ourselves cannot take place until the process is complete. You cannot put new wine into old bottles; and almost the first thing that we discover is how old the bottle is, thick, dense, dusty.

The training in Light continues; we find the texture of our minds changing; the angle of our vision is enlarged; a tiny thread of revealing Light is connected and permanently installed. You know how self-conscious one becomes when someone stares fixedly at any part of one's person, and one is convinced that something is wrong, and becomes

Revelation. The Revealing Power of the Light

uneasy in consequence. The revealing Light has the same effect on one's mind; it shows up, mercilessly, any shoddiness of texture. What the world, and sometimes even ourselves, has accepted as acts of virtue, the Light reveals as egotism. When we have been content to think carelessly and act unconsciously, we are inflexibly shown the difference between the standard of a conscious and an unconscious mind; and, having started on the Conscious Way, we can no longer avail ourselves of the those old light-hearted excuses. One used to think of oneself innocent of offence if unconsciously one caused offence. To sin in Light is to act unconsciously. Slowly the revealing Light does its work, transmuting the finite qualities of our mind into infinite attributes, gently, insidiously, inflexibly, preparing our humanity for the in-dwelling of the light body. If and when that happens we shall have installed another receiving station, and the Light of revelation can again function in man, as it functioned in Christ and His apostles.

Light must reveal man to himself; must transmute the condition of his mind; must test the quality of his desire before he can be trusted with the knowledge of its power; before he can become a steward of infinite mysteries. Power. That is the quest of mortal man in this world. It is also the quest of the soul in the next. Power to do great things, and power to be great. To achieve greatness in this world must be spectacular. The urge in man is to dominate his circumstances, to get out of the rut of the average intelligence, to have brains that will make money, talents that can be turned into gold, for money means material power. This longing to have power to achieve greatness would be a perfectly legitimate quest, if only it were superseded by the greater urge to *be* great. Here lies the kernel of the struggle between the finite and the infinite qualities of the mind.

There is infinite power in the knowledge of Light. In the world of Light you are known by the quality of light that radiates out from your light body. There can be no masquerading, no borrowing of garments, no touching up of wings. Here, one can hide one's feelings, appear different to what one is; one can self-consciously conceal one's virtues, and cloak vice with the mantle of charm. There, the soul body and the garment are one. If we have not been enriched by our earth life with spiritual experiences, if there has been no attempt to establish any connection with our future destination, then we go over with the barest outfit in life, just our light bodies. The spirit having failed to control the mind, must now prepare for another incarnation, drawing to itself all the power and knowledge that it can, to equip itself sufficiently for its next endeavour. Those who pass out of life with the highest distinctions in Light are those who have loved greatly. The soul body, as I have said, is a fragment fashioned from the substance of the Creator, and God is Love. Therefore, the spirit of man who loves greatly is always feeding and strengthening his light body. If he loves and serves humanity, as great souls in every profession do, he subjugates his body for the good of the cause he serves. His spirit, having been enriched by his earth experiences, passes on and finds his light body able to function in harmony and efficiency in more entrancing conditions than if he had spent his human energy on self-advancement and self-love. We must all go to that condition in Light where our own quality in Light enables us to live, and we are with those whose power is of the same calibre as our own. We cannot live here in grand houses on minute incomes; and over there we cannot live beyond the means of Light that we have accumulated during our last earth experience.

I have begun to realise what this world urge for power really signifies. It seems to me to be the inarticulate surging-up in the individual of the knowledge of his potential possibilities for domination. It must find expression, and not knowing the way of Light, it finds its outlet in darkness, resulting in deeds of violence, and all the horror that the human mind can invent to assist it in asserting its uninspired human authority.

"Not by might, nor by power, but by my spirit, saith the Lord of Hosts." How much nearer we are today to the understanding of that truth, than were the people of those old prophetic times, it is hard to calculate. Recent events are not encouraging, but they must at least crystallise to a decisive point in our minds as to where the thought of the world is

Revelation. The Revealing Power of Light

trending. Is it towards material power? Is it towards the divine? There is not a shadow of doubt but that it is the quest for power. It is world struggle between those who have a vision of world peace, and those who desire to hold fast in their human grasp the control of world's destinies. In reality, the controlling factor of the mind on the human side is fear, on the infinite side is love; and world strife is only the universal expression of the individual problem. The solution of the problem, therefore, lies with the individual.

It is hard, sometimes, not to indulge in day-dreams, and to visualise what this world could be like if the heads of the governments of the various nations were all conscious souls; had all fused their finite minds with their infinite egos; could all make an instant and direct contact with infinite power. It will come, this union in Light; this power to *be* great; this quality of the spirit that transcends the finest calibre of brain; this fusion with eternal power that enabled humble fishermen to leave their nets and to work miracles. It will come through knowledge, which is achieved by certainty of technique, individual experience, and freedom of expression. For we must have reality. Gold and all the lovely things in life that it can buy, is real. Light is real. We know how gold is tested. We learn how Light tests us. It transmutes the dross of our minds, it clarifies the human vessel, until it is, in very truth, able to receive the sacramental wine of revelation.

THE LAW OF TRANSMUTATION

Lecture delivered March 8th, 1934

This is yet another attempt to pass on to you the teaching I have received concerning transcendental conditions.

In four lectures given between 1930 and 1934 I have endeavoured to share with you different aspects of this teaching in Light.

The first, on Conscious Mediumship, I told you how it all started; how I, consciously, went through old initiations - part of the Egyptian and part of the Hermetic - experiencing again the ancient knowledge of magical and spiritual forces. In using the word "magic," I want you to eliminate from your minds, the adjective "black".

We have, in these superficial days, a loose method of thinking, and a still more casual way of talking, and the word "magic" invariably conjures up in our minds evil practices and secret rites of a sinister nature. But in the days to which I am alluding, the men who learnt the laws of the earth, or magical forces, were priests, and by the secret ritual of their inspiration they were able to fuse in harmony of operations the various rays of energy, impinging on, and emanating from the earth. They were the scientists of their civilisation. Electricity and wireless are the magic of the twentieth century; and the black side of modern magic is poison gas, torpedoes, and aerial bombs - forces of destruction, that strike fear into the hearts of men. There always has been knowledge of how to transmute substances for constructive or destructive ends. In this knowledge is contained the power to cure, the power to kill, the souls and bodies of the human race; and whether it is called science or magic, the power is the same, though its manifestation differs with each civilisation.

The important point that emerged out of that experience of receiving direct into my conscious understanding, the knowledge of the old initiations, was the certainty that no knowledge is lost; but, in the appointed time, it is superseded. We shall never progress by looking backwards. Excavations establish truth, and confirm theories but can

The Law of Transmutation

never reveal future experiences.

In the next lecture, which was called "The Worship of Light," I recorded various experiences obtained through psychometrising old stones. On these ancient sites, the old ritual lived again and clarified my conviction that knowledge of the laws of Light was, and is, and is to come.

The third lecture - "The Freedom of Two Worlds" - dealt with my dawning understanding of the past, the present, and the future condition of the soul; with the achievement of the Christ in fusing, in His human body, the laws of Light and of matter; and in demonstrating in His resurrection, the transcendental Law of Transmutation.

In my last lecture, entitled "Revelation," I enlarged, as far as I could, on the fact that this teaching provides the way of experience; and that it is only through the individual experience that divine revelation is apprehended.

And now, this fifth, and (I think) last lecture of the series, is an attempt to touch, as it were, the hem of His garment, and endeavour to bring within the scope of our comprehension the knowledge of the power that this Law of Transmutation gives to man. For it is the Law of Manifestation.

In ancient days, alchemy was an established science. The formulae were generally in the secret possession of individual alchemists, and their researches provided the experience of a life time.

On one of my psychometrising expeditions, I came, quite unexpectedly on an alchemist's stone. On our way south from Scotland, we stopped at an old Roman village (Uriconium, near Shrewsbury) which had been extensively excavated. As none of us had been there before, and as we were not pressed for time, we went to look at it, with no thought of psychometry in our minds. Like steel to a magnet I was drawn to a stone placed on mound in one of the numerous small dug-outs which show the foundation walls of the various residences. It necessitated my clambering down a wall, and climbing up the mound, on which there was barely room for me to crouch, and I did not know till I felt it in what lay its attraction for me.

The Trail

There was a slit on the top of the stone in which it was just possible for me to get the tips of my fingers. As I worked, pressing my hand down as far as I could, slowly the picture of an old man came, and I knew he was engaged in a trade that brought people into his place, and that he pursued quite openly his secret researches, and was never suspected of being an alchemist because of his trade. I got quite vividly this mixing of minute quantities of very precious substances, with the greatest care and accuracy, and I got very thrilled and wished I could have pressed my fingers further down, as I knew there was something left there which I could not make a contact with. And then I knew that the formula had gone for ever, that the cypher had been burnt.

It is not often that I get corroboration as promptly as I did that day. For, going round the place we talked to a man who had helped to excavate. On asking him if he knew what the place was where the stone stood, and and if it had any connection with the spot where it was standing, he told us that it was thought to be a blacksmith's forge. A large furnace had been unearthed, and the stone was near it; in that furnace they had discovered many crucibles of various sizes. The point of extraordinary interest for me was the fact that they had found several minute crucibles, so tiny that they could not imagine for what purpose they had been used. He then took us round the small museum, and showed us the microscopic little containers, and I recognised at once that they, or ones similar to them, had held the precious fragments that my alchemist had worked on. I seemed to know that he was a metal worker, and not a blacksmith; and that, as an expert craftsman he was able to carry out his experiments quite unsuspected by his clients. We also learnt that the town had been entirely destroyed by fire.

I had another interesting experience at this same place. We were walking round the grounds, and I suddenly stopped, arrested by the sound of women's voices. They were chattering and laughing; and I, too, burst out laughing. It all seemed so gay, and though I couldn't really understand the words, I somehow knew the meaning, and they were gossiping and joking and being most amusing.

The Law of Transmutation

Afterwards we learnt that I was standing at the entrance of what was called "the hall of conversation," leading to the Roman ladies' baths!

The intonation of those women's voices is there now, as fresh and as strong as in the time when they all chattered and laughed together.

Two episodes - the first being the record in stone of the science of alchemy. The alchemist's stone was but the prelude to our modern factories, where synthetic gold can be produced, where milk may be transmuted into eronoid, where substances can be changed and form altered. Alchemy has developed into industry, and magic into science; but that aspect of the Law of Transmutation which changes the spirit and substance of man, has been demonstrated, but has never been technically developed; and it is that aspect of the Law that I desire to deal with now.

The secret researches of modern scientists are largely concerned with the elimination of the germs of disease in the blood. What are the future generations going to say of the researches of man of today? They will read the records of the sacrifice of monkeys, rabbits, guinea-pigs and rats on the altar (or dissecting table) of the god of health. Will they see a vast difference between the expression of science and the manifestation of magic? Or the sacrifice of bulls and heifers to Jehovah?

Down all the centuries comes this investigation into the power of the blood - this link between the expression of finite and infinite life. There are many rituals concerned with blood rites that are practised in some races in different parts of the world today; and there is a profound knowledge in the biological world of the functionary power of blood. The key to the understanding of this Law of Transmutation lies in the comprehension of the ingredients of the blood. It rests with the biologists to supply, as it were, the keyhole, but it should be through the inspiration of the spiritual scientist to fit the key. If man were wholly human, science could evolve a completely healthy body, by eliminating the disease germs from the blood, and also supplying the blood with the ingredients it lacks, thus ensuring a healthy circulation. Man, however, being partly divine, has that Life Principle in his blood that no doctor can revitalize once the heart ceases to beat. He must, therefore, look to the divine specialist to supply the missing link.

It was by the power in His blood, that Jesus, the Christ, based His claim to His divine attributes. There was that substance, He said, in His blood, which had power to save the whole world. A pretty big claim; and one, of course, repudiated by His ignorant enemies. The man who, through his research work, discovered the use of insulin, had power to save those suffering from diabetes from inevitable death, and results justified his claim. It can only be by results that claims are established.

This teaching does not overlap the biological researches into the functioning power of the blood, but it does, most certainly, dovetail into it.

We are, with the exception of the medical profession, extraordinarily ignorant concerning the activities of our own life-supply. We cannot keep it free from invading germs. We suffer from bad circulation and all its attendant evils; but above all we do experience in our blood the results of our emotional reactions. Fear, that may paralyse our movements; hate, that may cause apoplexy; frustration of expression, that is the cause of so many nervous diseases; and violent passions, which provide every form of congestion. Science is often able to prevent a potential disease from developing, but it is quite unable to prevent the emotions from poisoning the system. Ignorant and unobservant as we are of the effect of our mind processes on our bodies, we are nevertheless entirely responsible for our emotional reactions. We live in a practical age, in a century that is discarding orthodox shibboleths. It is useless telling young people of today not to do things that they wish to do, without providing them with a sufficiently good reason to justify the prohibition. We have an extensive ethical doctrine of Christian behaviour, and Christian doctrines; but we are given no technique to develop our capacity to achieve the ideal set before us. "Control yourself," "Control your tongue," we are told. Yes, but how? Pray, quite true - but what is prayer? Is there really power in the repetition of words? If I pray for rain - will it rain? If I pray to be made good, will I be good? It sounds so easy, but it just does not happen. It is no good controlling my anger, it does not change it. I'm not good, because I control my badness. I seem good; but

The Law of Transmutation

I, knowing myself, know that I am exactly the same, and self-control has not changed my intolerance - my tongue longs to say that last destructive word. To transmute our emotional processes is not to control them, but to change them; and all change is subject to law, and technical knowledge of law must result in demonstration. Controlled fear is not courage; but fear transmuted is fearlessness.

Controlled hate is not love; but one can transmute hate into love.

I have learnt that this spiritual Law of Transmutation is one of the laws of Light; that this particular Light energy functions as certainly and as accurately on our spirits, as does that law function which transmutes the proper proportion of hydrogen and oxygen gas into water. Once you know the technique it provides the same certainty. The corrosive power of lime cannot act differently to the law of its being, and there are as many immutable conditions in Light as there are in matter. No law can be demonstrated without the necessary conditions for manifestation. So, the Law of Transmutation could never have been demonstrated if the Christ had not offered Himself as the subject for the divine experiment. If He had done it alone; if He had left no example of His technique behind, it would have remained the eternal enigma. But it is precisely in the demonstrations of His twelve pupils, drawn from various trades and professions, whom He personally taught, that we have the living record of His technique.

When He was alive, and lived with them, they watched Him; often speculated amongst themselves; criticized and doubted. They were amazed at the constant proofs He gave of the reality of His assertions; and, finally, they proved sufficiently to work, occasionally, on their own initiative. The emphasis of the fact that He worked by law is provided by the actions of His pupils after His death.

The Law of the Transmutation of the substance of matter into the substance of Light had been triumphantly manifested in what is known as the Resurrection.

We have all consciously reincarnated, whether we realise the fact or not; but nobody before or since the Christ has so mastered the law of life in matter that they have foretold their power to consciously disintegrate their atoms, and the time necessary for the achievement. The fact that He foretold His death and conscious resurrection, in a way that would not impede its accomplishment, made it possible, afterwards, to understand the expediency of His early death. It was essential that He should have living witnesses to testify to the fact that He had fulfilled His promise to inspire them to work by the laws that He had demonstrated to the world. It was absolutely necessary to prove that the same works could be done, if the same conditions were observed.

It is intensely interesting to note the difference in the capacities of the twelve men, after His death; the amazing certainty of their achievements. They, who had doubted, had been full of fears, had been so aware of the power of Rome, were now inspired by the very attributes of the Christ — courage, selflessness, love, service, knowledge.

Down the ray of pure inspiration was the conscious mind of the Christ manifested in His pupils, by the same method by which He had been inspired; with identically the same power, and with identically the same results.

By far the most striking example of this method was, of course, Paul of Tarsus. In him we have of the Law of Transmutation most perfectly expounded.

He has his vision in Light. So great and blinding a radiance is it, that he is completely dazed. He is singled out - not because of his merit - but because of his capacity. His very revulsion towards the Nazarene, his pride of race, his ruthless energy, his authority vested in Caesar - were all attributes of antagonism to love. The quality of his mind was to provide the necessary substance to prove the working of the Law of Transmutation. The vision came in Light; and along the ray of wisdom came experience, and we see Paul learning humbly how to transmute the destructive qualities of his strong and passionate nature into a constructive scheme of life. If only all those who listened to his expounding of the Law had taken the next step and experienced the truth of its functioning power the world would be peopled with supermen today.

The Law of Transmutation

But they listened to him, and apprehended with their minds, and the knowledge of the Law was kept; but the experiencing of it was lost.

The light traffic-signals are the result of co-operative organisation, which has succeeded in establishing a new condition of behaviour for vehicles and pedestrians; experience has established that condition as law. The blind man is aware of the law; but, by reason of his blindness he cannot experience the observance of it. That is the nearest analogy I can submit to the functioning of the spiritual laws of Light. The Law of Transmutation established a new condition of behaviour in the conscious spirit, and the experiences become the law of their being; changing the congested, erratic, uncertain condition into a free, certain and rhythmic co-operation. The unconscious spirit may mentally apprehend the law; but, by reason of his unconscious condition, is unable to experience the observance of it. Mental knowledge of that law does not change our condition, unless we co-operate in the experiencing of it.

I cannot sufficiently stress the fact of the difference between learning and experience. There have been many wise teachers and philosophers who have had a very lofty mental ideal of the behaviour of life; and when the opportunity to demonstrate the truth of their mental apprehension is provided, their spirit has been unable to stand the test of experience.

We have, in the example of Christ's life, the manifestation of the law. He did not only preach the law of love; He demonstrated it. He did not only talk of His power to transmit the power of God, He showed them that power in action, not as a condition peculiar to Himself, but what should be a universal manifestation. It was extraordinarily difficult for Him to simplify this great transcendental truth. If the people could but understand that, if they transmuted the hardness of their hearts, the blindness of their vision, their inertia, into intelligent co-operation, then they would be able to understand the technicalities of the law as comprehensively as He did. Nothing could prevent it from functioning except the lack of co-operation. It was with such urgency that He said to them that, if they couldn't believe merely because He told them it was true, then let the manifestation speak for itself. Deeds must convince, when words have failed to do so.

But, the same conditions prevailed then, as they do now. They simply could not believe that His experiences could be theirs. The same excuses were offered then as they are today. So busy - in the home, in business, in society; poor health - so little time. How much nearer in experience are we than the people of His day? How much have we studied His technique? How often have we, individually, heard it stated that Christianity is dead, finished, and that the world needs a new revelation? What is the assertion based on? Is it because we have assimilated into our being the knowledge and experience of the law of love, so that, in the world today, there is such a superfluity of Christ-men that the type is standardised, and that we must reach out for a high ideal for attainment?

We know that this is not true, we know that we have not yet begun to function in perfect equilibrium of mind and spirit and body, and the secret of our failure is that we have no burning desire to do so.

The ideal of a public schoolboy is not to be a Christ at thirty, but to be prime minister at twenty-two; and what mother, desiring her son to be a super-man, has cherished any real desire for him to follow in the footsteps of the real Super-Man?

Looking back down the centuries, what figure stands out in history on such a peak of unattainable achievement as the man Jesus? And what group of pioneers have attained such world wide notoriety, have blazed so limitless a trail, as the twelve who learnt from Him? Their words and experiences, inspiration and manifestations, have never yet been ethically or scientifically superseded.

Through that experience of hearing the Roman ladies' amusing gossip, I have learned a very great truth. No learned treatise on the wavelengths of sound would have convinced me of the possibility of the earth retaining (as surely as a gramophone record retains) the ejection of sound from the human vocal cords. Nor would I have known that the atmospheric conditions do not impinge on the earth laws. However

The Law of Transmutation

plausible a scientific theory may be, the experience of the manifestation of law incorporates into one's being the certainty of its functioning power, and one becomes part of the knowledge of creation. I realised what a focusing point for power the human individual can be, fusing in his being knowledge of finite and infinite laws; and I realised that all infinite wisdom must be experienced before it can be taught. That the word, or sound of creative force, must be ejected through the human agent before the sound can be retained in the earth.

The whole progress of the creative scheme seemed to clarify in my mind. Who could manifest the Law of Transmutation to the suffering world? Who could set the traffic signals, so that out of congestion and uncertainty, experience of the Law might be achieved? Who was great enough? Who could love enough?

What the world needs today is a technique to acquire transcendental power. Power to transmute our vulnerability to the devitalizing conditions of this twentieth century. The source of human vitality lies in the blood. The aim of modern alchemy is to change the substance of the blood, to transmute is absorbed impurities, which provide the decaying principle of the flesh, into a vital, untainted stream of creative energy. There is also in the blood, the eternal life principle; namely, the quickening of the blood, the essence of life itself. When that is withdrawn at death, it causes the blood to congeal and the flesh to decay. What known element is there, in the world today, that can come and go, with a swiftness unmeasurable in time? LIGHT! Light is the germ of life; life and Light are interchangeable terms.

The time is coming when the biologists will be able to discern in the blood this atom of eternal essence, but they will be helpless to increase the quantity, until they turn to the records left by the students of the Great Physician, who demonstrated to them in private, and manifested in public, the fact that in His words and in His deeds lay the secret power of His blood.

He knew how to draw direct into His being the invisible rays of transcendental power. He experienced the Law of Transmutation of His spirit, making His human body the focusing point, so that His blood was able to absorb, to a superlative degree, this essence of our eternal counterpart. When the process of absorption was accomplished, He was able to transmit a radiating force of such stupendous voltage, that, when ejected into the being of one in whom the spirit of Light had left the body, He was able to quicken into activity the life principle of the blood.

The technique that enabled Him to achieve this miracle was given to Him, He affirmed, direct from the Father of Light, and He, in turn, passed it on to the twelve. Paul had it second-hand from them, and was enabled to achieve his own experience and to demonstrate the Law.

This method of learning, established by the divine teacher for His pupils was inspirational and telepathic, identical with the procedure of His own initiation. That method holds good today, for all those willing to be initiated into the process. The understanding of the mystery of the infinite substance of the blood can be achieved by technical knowledge. It will enable us to make a contact with the rays of transcendental Light, which, passing through us, can be transmitted to the world.

That power was focused and transmitted by the Christ, and is in the world today.

The laughter of those Roman ladies' voices ripples still, though the walls have gone, and only the earth remains. And the sound of "The Word" is in the world today, though the flesh is not. The power remains; and, I maintain, has never been superseded.

"ALL I HAVE TO GIVE"

An Address given on Trinity Sunday, May 27th, 1934

Today is Trinity Sunday - the day set apart by enlightened people to seek revelation concerning their conception of God.

God created us; and, in return, we create His image - His likeness - and, far more often, His caricature.

No man hath seen God; it can only be from the angle of man's vision that we can get a reflection of that great radiance. A prison window gives the minimum of light; and a glass-house gives the maximum. A small, bitter, warped, egotistical mind gives the minimum radiation of the greatness of God. The selfless, wise, gentle, just, lovable mind glorifies the divine attributes in Him, and the reality of God is manifested. Therefore, the knowledge of the beingness of God depends on the manifestation of man.

Down all the ages great spirits have incarnated and taken on human limitations, in a selfless endeavour to give the world some greater conception of divine wisdom, power, or love than had been accomplished before: and every time the finite and infinite world was drawn a little closer together. Down those human links a pathway was made which rendered possible the incarnation of the great spirit of the Christ - the Light of the world. He revealed, for the first time, the living oneness of God. For He knew God. He was His only son. So He came to give us an intimate picture of the incomprehensible, in which the awe, the majesty, the power, the tenderness, tolerance, and integrity of the Father was described and manifested. It was a personal revelation of a personal experience. He was all He had to give, and He gave His all.

He was not a symbol of Light. He was the Light. Of the same substance as the Father; for sons and fathers are always of the same substance. You must remember that 2,000 years ago, the people did not know the power of light as we do today. They had no search-lights; no radiant advertisements; no dimming and blazing of motor headlamps; no parables that could convey to their minds the familiar conditions of the sudden darkness occasioned by a broken fuse; or the instantaneous radiation made possible by the turning of a switch. Only a sense of remoteness would have been enhanced had He likened the Father to the starry constellations. For centuries God had been worshipped as the Sun behind the sun. And now came Jesus who dared to say that to know Him the Nazarene was to know God. The wise men knew this truth. Wise men have always sought for the manifestation of God in man - by man - and through man. The quality of His love in man; the manifestation of His power by man; and the knowledge of the cosmos that is transmitted through man. And that trinity of the unity of God was revealed to the world by the manifestation of Jesus.

The divinity of Christ has been a difficult problem for many people; but knowledge of the laws of Light reveal the truth. He was both man and God. His body was of the same substance of man; flesh and blood. His spirit was of that incandescent quality of Light that makes a contact with the essence of Light - not a concussion, but a fusion: not a syncopation in Light, such as our spirits make when in contrary rhythm to the rhythm of God, for He knew how to tune in so that His being fused in the oneness and the harmony of the life pulse, or rhythm, of God.

Do you begin to see what divinity really is? Oneness in Light. What we, as children of Light, have got to understand is that the divinity of Jesus Christ, His oneness with God, did not make Him less but more human; because only in His relationship to God can we understand His humanity. His incarnation was a two-fold accomplishment; the perfecting of the human, finite, substance of flesh by the fusion with the eternal infinite substance of Light. It made Him completely vulnerable on the human side; for though His spirit knew, His human mind had to learn; His body had to experience. He had in Him the capacity for failure on the human side; but His spirit was free of the karmic law - of past sin. There was no quality of expiation. There was no disharmony of law in His spirit; therefore He was free of sin. The body does not sin; it is merely the vehicle for the expression of our spirits, and our minds are the

"All I Have to Give"

deciding factors for manifestation. That is why St. Paul said - "Let this mind be in you, that was also in Christ Jesus." It must be our endeavour to achieve "the mind of Christ," His mind which directed the activities of His body. Instead we are often content with an attempted imitation of His actions, lacking the inspiration that He had of the knowledge of the mystery of divine unity. The key to that mystery lay in personal experience. His spirit had pierced through the denseness of a mortal mind, and He maintained that His example could be followed by all who desired to tread in His footsteps; and why they faltered and turned aside was, that they thought that following Him meant repetition of experience, that only by being despised and rejected on earth could you be great in heaven. They failed, as we have failed in the succeeding centuries, to realise that unless Jesus had manifested the love of God in circumstances that made Him the object of contempt, hate and mob hysteria we could never have known that there is no social outcast in all the wide world who cannot, if he follow Christ, become too a son of God. The Christ was then the only spirit that achieved complete domination of material conditions through spiritual power; and will remain for ever the first-born son. But that truth must never obscure the gift that He, as God's almoner came to give the world; that, as many as received Him, to them gave He power to become the sons of God.

    The desire to possess this power is the secret yearning of the hearts of men. He knew it; and so He, in utter selflessness, provided the way of escape from the karmic law. A living way; not the way of the recluse - the hermit - the dreamer - or the philosopher. Not enough to know the mysteries. The Pharisees - the Sadducees - all the masters in Israel - were students and adepts in the ancient and modern sciences of their day; as was the Christ Himself. He knew their laws. There is a vast difference between the knowledge and the expert demonstration of a law. Mentally, we can apprehend all of Christ's teaching; but we cannot demonstrate it. He knew we could not, unless we learnt the way. So, now, in the twentieth century, through the reincarnated experiences of past lives, men's minds have been prepared to receive the sacramental wine of life. He asked His disciples of old: "Are ye able to drink the cup that I drink?" and they said: "We are able." And He said: "My cup indeed ye shall drink." He asks us today: "Can ye drink?" and we answer: "Yea, Lord."

This way is the way of the Christian Initiate. We can be given the power to become the sons of God; and that is the inscription on the first step of the initiate's path; and on the last step is written: "They that are led by the spirit of God, they are the sons of God."

To be led by the spirit of God is to be controlled, directed, and obedient to that quality of divine power that enabled Jesus to transmute His human mind, to become invulnerable to the impingement of the orthodox traditional Jewish laws of His day; and to keep inviolate in utter certainty the inspiration that proceeded from the mind of God.

We know that it is possible to make a contact with the minds of those we love who pass on. The Spiritualist Movement has established experience of individual survival; and, great as this work has been, it is, as it were, but the opening of the lodge gates, that lead to the palace of the king. Once inside those gates, the park is there for rest and enjoyment. But those who desire to be presented to the king do not linger, interesting though it may be to see rare shrubs and plants that do not grow outside, where the soil is different. But they press on, finding that the path leads away from the open park; it is not an easy way to find - many doors seem to have no way of opening; for the palace of the king must be guarded from sight-seers, advertising agents, and profiteers. But there is a right-of-way - leading through the palace into the private gardens behind. Only one person has ever voluntarily left the lovely place; going through the palace, He left the door open, and, passing through the park, gave instructions to the lodge that all who knocked should be admitted; and all who desired to see His Father should be allowed to find their own way in. For He was laying a trail of Light, that could instantly be picked up by those who had eyes to see. He wandered through the world, laying His invisible trail, the hounds of darkness on His track. He accomplished His work. For the quality of His love transmuted the quality of weariness.

"All I Have to Give"

That long, lonely trail, without a mortal mind to help or understand. How different it is for us. We have only to pick it up; and the finding of His footsteps must be an individual experience. Having found the trail, we can share, and pass the knowledge on. We can say to those in the park: "Come on; we have found the trail. You are not at the end of the journey because you have passed through the outer gates."

That is why these lectures have been published, for all that I have to give is just this — knowledge that has been revealed to me of the trail of Light that the Christ laid, that leads direct to the presence of the Father.

HUMAN DOCUMENT

THE RECONSTRUCTION OF THE INDIVIDUAL

SEQUEL TO *THE TRAIL*

By

OLIVE C.B. PIXLEY

Copyright
The Armour of Light Trust Council

First Published 1947
Revised Publication 1999

FOREWORD

It is just over twenty years ago since my training in the Christian Initiation started. The account of those experiences was made public and printed in a little book entitled *The Trail*. It briefly recorded the initiations of a neophyte into the ancient rituals of the worship of Light, in the Egyptian, Hermetic and Mithraic priesthood. It ended by stressing that the Christian Initiation embodied all the old truth and carried forward into the every day of modern life a new message for all peoples of every race and every creed. The founder, Jesus Christ, put no barriers of a social cast, no sex superiority, no age limit. If one had ears, one could hear, if one had eyes, one could see. Ears to hear the pattern of the plan, eyes to see the demonstration. I hope in the following pages to give an account of a group of people who are following the trail left two thousand years ago by the Christ.

The problem of the day is, how can the world win the peace? Conferences dealing with the work of reconstruction are in being, and there is so much good will but so little experience. It is obvious that there will be no lasting peace until we realise that world reconstruction depends on individual reconstruction, and that until human nature changes, the world remains eternally the same; therefore war must be the inevitable recurring factor for the annihilation of human life and prosperity.

Christ came to free the world from blind obedience to the "letter of the law". There was only one way of doing it, and that was to demonstrate how to become the Law. Becoming the Law is not a matter of words or intoning, it is experience and works. The capacity for experience is universally the same, the actual experience must be individually different.

The proof of the accuracy of any formula lies in its functioning power. The proof of the formula that Christ enunciated, to love God and to love one's neighbour and to forgive one's enemies, was demonstrated by Him as a working proposition. He also gave exact directions by which these works could be achieved. Those directions have been ignored, so the works have not been accomplished by the church as an institution. Therefore Christianity as an institution is dead. Christ as an individual is still alive. The reconstruction or resurrection of the living Christ in all races is of paramount importance. How is the universal contact to be made? Obviously not through the intellect, equally obviously it must be through the co-ordination of the heart and mind.

The heart is supposed to be the emotional centre, and therefore distrusted by the intellect. Actually all emotion is a cerebral reaction affecting the heart action, but not instituted by it. The brain was created to be the receiving instument of transcendental truth, and the heart to circulate and transmit the life energy. The brain and heart control all organic functions, the key therefore to the eternal health or the dictatorship of death lies in the focus of the individual mind.

The training of the mind to focus demands a technique. That Technique was revealed to me twenty years ago, and I was shown that Light is life energy, and that by accepting quite simply my ignorance concerning modern scientific terminology, the cosmic pattern of life in visible and also invisible matter could be apprehended by and demonstrated through the most ordinary of individuals, namely myself. Today there are many witnesses to testify that what started as a thrilling individual experience is becoming an enthralling universal certainty. The Technique in Light is now available for anyone who, reading the following testimony, desires to devote their service to reconditioning their physical instrument, thus enabling them to transmit effortlessly, eternal life.

Our blood always radiates to our neighbour the substance of ourselves, our disharmonies of living radiate out as diseases, our harmony diffuses its aura of joy and is equally infectious.

If we want to follow in Christ's footsteps, we can. I stress the word footsteps, for the brain being the receiving set, the heart the transmitter and the feet are the earth, and without the earth the transmission is bound to be faulty.

The Christian Initiate dedicates his brain, his heart and his feet.

Foreword

The Technique in Light trains the initiate into receiving the life energy, which expands his comprehension and transmutes his physical substance, and he becomes inevitably a channel through whom the Christ can work the miracles this generation is so greatly in need of.

There is a training centre, where classes are held (free) for the learning of the Technique in Light, and where the channels gain experience in healing. There is also a correspondence course for the Technique so that those who cannot come to the classes may get the training by post.

Finally I need to explain that this is not a book but a document of human experience and is the substance of revelation. It has been written for the purpose of making known the fact that the fusion of the Christ's consciousness with that of the ordinary individual can become a universal experience.

Olive C.B. Pixley
13 Ashburn Place
London S.W.7
(1947)

This narrative is dedicated to Jack and to Jill.
                    (J.N.F.P.)   (J.R.D.)

In Beauty is all Love,
In Love is all Service,
In Service is all Joy,
In Joy is perfect Stillness,
And in that Stillness
                I Am.

Human Document

PART I

THE SON OF MAN

Page

Chapter	I.	Foundation	.....	111
Chapter	II.	Illusion	.....	117
Chapter	III.	Perspective	.....	125
Chapter	IV.	Distinction	.....	132
Chapter	V.	Before and After	.....	136
Chapter	VI.	Today	.....	144

PART II

THE CHRISTIAN INITIATION 150

Chapter I.

FOUNDATION

When a house is rebuilt, it is necessary to examine the foundations to ascertain their ability to stand and withstand the weight and strain of the building that is to be erected. The same detailed process must take place in the reconstruction of the individual. One must examine the foundation of one's certainties, for certainty is the only substance which can be used as a foundation stone on which to build the new temple. That temple is the body, not built by hands as are churches, but built by character, which is an indestructible substance. Some temples are built on the sands of emotion, shifting, cracking and finally crumbling under the stress of catastrophe. Others are built on the wooden platform of inherited tradition and when the dry rot of worn out symbolism attacks it, it has no power of resistance and crumbles into dust.

So few people believe that when Jesus talked of His flesh and blood He really meant it. That when He talked of the body as a temple, He meant exactly what He said. To rebuild a body is a life's work, for the process of reconstruction must be cell by cell and organ by organ. One cannot start rebuilding unless one has as one's foundation the certain belief in the resurrection of the body. Not a celestial body but a physical one, "For as in Adam all die even so in Christ shall all be made alive." In man alone is the process of decay and death of physical matter. Christ came to demonstrate a method by which the process of reconstruction should take place during the life time. He had to die because He had to take on sub-normal man, to transform His sub-normality into the normality of perfect manhood. He had publicly to demonstrate the exact condition of death which is the separation of the human mind from God. In those words "My God, my God, why hast thou forsaken me," He exposes for all time the error into which the mind of the human race had fallen - namely making God responsible for the separation. Separation from God is death, unity with God is life.

All His life Christ had identified Himself with His Father and in that identification of unity of substance had built into His flesh and blood the divine current of life energy. The foundation stone of His life was obedience. He could be obedient because of His certainty of His Father's ability to direct His every action, dominate every thought. If He had ever doubted His Father He would have been unable of Himself to accomplish His mission. That mission was the reconstruction of the physical body. To that purpose was He dedicated and step by step He freed Himself mentally from the prejudices, intolerances and rigidities of the creed of His race. The veil of illusion that hung across the threshold of the Holy of Holies had to be destroyed before the new era could be ushered in, before the resurrection of His body could be manifested. Faith is experience, knowledge is the substance of experience. Christ had to go through all human experiences to become the Law of Love in every fibre of His being. He had to be born as one of the masses to be able to love His neighbour as Himself. He had to have enemies to know how to love them. He had to be persecuted to experience forgiveness for cruelty and distortion of fact. Finally He had to experience absolute failure, loneliness and death to know for Himself that in death alone God has no part. He is not in death for Love is life.

That is Christ's unique achievement; transcending Egyptian, Hermetic and Mithraic experience. It was the establishing on earth of a new physical instrument capable of direct contact with cosmic energy. That instrument was His body, composed of flesh and blood, which He came to restore to its pre-Adamic capacity of perfect receptivity and transmission of the life force, constantly referred to as "eternal life". He endeavoured to educate the masses to comprehend the difference between the accepted limits of the life energy which animates the body of mortal man terminating in decay and death, and the capacity of the individual to receive and transmit the eternal flow of life force, by connecting up the living instrument with the source of all life in this world, the great Father God. The linking up of the instrument with the source was, He said, a voluntary action, it could not be affected by compulsion. Once connected, the result was inevitable and the reaction would be the same, whether in a

Foundation

child, in a priest, in a shepherd or a king. It was the law governing atomic energy.

The vested interests of the priesthood could not tolerate mass conversion and mass freedom. The moment the formula was understood by the intelligentsia, propaganda to destroy His rising popularity and belittle His activities started and has persisted to this day. His real mission has been wilfully obscured. His body, instead of being a living model has become a mystical relic and the intonation of His life's works a tedious repetition. He came that we should have life and have it more abundantly and we are treated to an endless contemplation of His death. His reconstruction of the living instrument, the perfecting of human capacity, the culminating triumph of scientific achievement is referred to in one single sentence but understood and believed in its fullest implication by very few. "On the third day He rose again and then ascended into heaven."

There is the formula, the experiment stood vindicated for the process of death was transcended, physical substance was now able to hold the voltage of eternal energy. Jesus transcended the law of gravitation and ascended out of visible range. He gave a new and living demonstration of a universal physical capacity; that it has remained a unique demonstration is not His fault but our shameful stupidity and inertia. As the body is controlled by the brain He could only leave an urgent request behind for those who cared to follow in His footsteps, "Remember Me." To remember is vital in all research work. A code is useless without a single mind that can remember how to use it.

Jesus gave the twelve at the last meal He had with them, a code that all could use wherever they were at all times. Knowing human nature as He did, He chose the evening meal for His time of remembrance; even if they forgot Him during the day, they should remember the human side of Him, food, real flesh, real blood, not mystical and remote, but solidly real to make the focal point for His re-appearance. If they would remember His humanity He could be human and they would attract Him to them.

He had to demonstrate how, by tuning in to His Father the connection was made and the works performed with unerring exactitude. If He focused His mind on the Father then the Father, through the dedicated body of the Son, could transmit this eternal energy and renew in an instantaneous flash the minus condition manifested by the individual. The Son drew from the Father — the patient drew from the Son. If the Son had forgotten or doubted the Father He could have done nothing greater than the hypnotists and medicos of His day. But because He knew how to draw into His own being the perfect energy and acknowledged publicly the source it never did or could fail Him.

Pilate would have had no power over Him unless He had voluntarily gone through His human experience. That He had a will of His own is certain. In Gethsemane when faced with the fact that, without a public death there could be no public resurrection, when the full implication was borne in on Him of the reaction on His friends and enemies, then His quick mind knew that not one of them would be able to "take" the crucifixion. As a man of the world He sought to suggest to His Father every other alternative method, and there was none. Then He audibly relinquished His will, "Not my will but Thine be done," and for all time has left the directions for universal freedom — absolute obedience, absolute confidence.

He achieved the reconstruction of His body and He became the Law. No longer was He subject to Caesar. He was different in aspect but He was aware of the reaction on the uninitiated and so He gave the warning, "Touch me not," for the atomic energy might have been too strong and they might have been shattered by the contact. In these early days He had not had time to provide an earth and consciously experience the working capacity of this new living instrument. Very soon it was working normally, eating, drinking, walking, talking and finally demonstrating His fourth dimensional activity, His power of "throughness". Now He could go through matter - a locked door was no barrier, provided the magnetic condition was strong enough to attract Him. The law of magnetic attraction in the blood was earthed. He now

Foundation

impressed the formula on His followers "Where two or three are gathered in My name, there am I in the midst of them." On them was laid the responsibility for materialisation. He was dependent on the magnetic currents of their heart's blood.

The heart is the organ that contains and controls the blood and therefore is of first importance in the Christian Initiation. The heart is the magnet that provides Love's visibility. The priests depended on the brain for imposing authority. They dominated the mind and inducing the infection of fear, caused the subjugation of the people by imposing the letter of the law, which was the hallmark of organised religion. No wonder this freelance of Love advocating fearless contact with supreme authority, who asked with certainty of receiving, who imposed no social barriers, who considered one man was as potentially good as another, was an anathema to the rigid disciplinarians of the Temple.

To achieve His objective He had voluntarily to submit to imposed authority. He had to prove that death was separation from life and that, if a conscious contact with the Father could be maintained, then there would be no death of physical substance. His oneness with God was so faithful, so uninterrupted that only in His last conscious moment did He, in a strong voice, so that all in the vicinity of the cross could hear, proclaim in evidence of His experience exactly what death was, this illusion of the human mind that God has the power to forsake man.

The moment the human mind declares the absence of God there is no life. God is life; identify yourself with Life and you are one with Life. God is Love; identify yourself with Love and you are Love. In man's mind is death; identify yourself with death and you die. In man's mind is fear; identify yourself with fear and you are afraid. One can go through all the attributes of God and man and know through one's individual experience the truth. We know that a few times in a life the individual identifies himself with God and miracles occur.

The problem that confronts the human race today is, how can the millions of minds, mass-educated to believe in the development of the ego, be changed into recognising their capacity to become a Christ? By the developing of their ego they can become a Hitler, by the eliminating of their *self*-consciousness they can become divine.

Chapter II.

ILLUSION

At the moment of Christ's public announcement that death is the illusion of the human mind, the veil of the Temple was rent. It is a cosmic impossibility that the magnet can withdraw from its own magnetism, or the sun dim its own brilliance. An object can remain outside the radius of the attracting power of the magnet or a material substance conceal the light of the sun. Because an individual sits in a dark room it does not affect the sun, but the darkness reacts on the individual and what use is the sun to the prisoner who never sees it?

What good does the statement "Be of good cheer for I have over-come the world" do for the man who does not believe in the reconstruction of the body? Christ destroyed the illusion of death by reconstructing His physical body. He could only have done that by consciously re-uniting Himself with the source of life, His Father God. He had to prove that if the human being is faithful to the instructions and trains his mind to focus on the Father, it would be physically impossible for him to be ill, poor, miserable, or for the body to decay. Separate the mind from its focus and the body becomes a prey to fear, ill health and death. The Holy of Holies is the place of the presence of truth. That place of revelation was veiled, rightly, from all except the true initiate. That veil symbolises the illusion that prevents the ordinary man from entering into the place of revelation. Fact destroys illusion.

Jesus invited the masses into the Holy of Holies, if they would voluntarily subscribe to the necessary conditions that would immediately open the door. The instructions were simple. Focus the mind and heart on the Father and put your neighbour on an equal basis with yourself. He put those directions into operation and the results were miraculous. But He did nothing else: He had nothing up His sleeve, as it were, that would ensure His success. His mind held no illusions, it was focused on His Father, as if He were always at the end of the telephone listening to a long distance call. His ear was the apparatus. He was always listening in. His mind thus focused on the mind of the Father, became a perfect receiving set, directing His actions and revitalising His body.

What I want to stress is this, that Christ's body could not have died unless He had willingly gone through the experience of total mental separation. His mind tuning in to human mental illusion, voiced its agony, and in that moment the human race was given the opportunity to transcend illusion. Perhaps the airmen of today with their complicated mechanism of "inter-communication" in the air, when they listen to a voice giving them instructions how to land in safety, will be able to realise more simply than others the line of communication set up by Jesus direct to celestial G.H.Q. How dense we have been these 2,000 years in ignoring what a perfect instrument the body is for the most exciting of all experiments, for the receiving instead of destroying Life. One of the chief illusions of the questioning mind is this: why, if we were meant to know, did not Christ give more explicit directions? Why didn't He leave a technique behind that would ensure His acts being repeated and developed?

If we look for the key for the mystery, we shall inevitably find it. Faith, He said, was the substance out of which miracles are fashioned. Faith is the substance of experience. Jesus had faith in God, because He had experience of His efficiency. After all, God had created matter; He was therefore a materialist and an expert. He had created the human body; therefore He must know how the thing worked and what the maximum capacity of the creature was. It was only logical that when Jesus embarked on His adventure into the world created by God, with whom He was on intimate terms, and with whom He had for aeons past discussed and planned the adventure, that He should have established lines of communication so that, in all matters relating to the enlightenment of the human race concerning its high destiny, He should have expert advice whenever He needed it.

No wonder He was stern with the propaganda chiefs, the Scribes, Pharisees and Sadduces, those brilliant minds stubbornly set against a new technique. He could not force it across the rigid limits of their mental apprehension. Always they looked back. What had been should be.

Illusion

They wanted nothing new. They had made Jehovah in their own image. They knew His moods. They could manage Him perfectly and as His representatives, enjoy the power He invested in them. Such a state of affairs was far too satisfactory to be renounced.

Jesus was notably far more severe on mental prostitution than on physical adultery. The first put stumbling blocks deliberately in the way of the ignorant and for that there was no excuse. The second was an act of individual self-indulgence for which the individual would be called to account. People are misled into thinking that because Jesus did not condemn, He condoned. Another illusion. He was the Law of Love. He had no power to condemn any act that came from the heart however ill-advised it might be for the person concerned. The deliberate falsifying of truth and the deliberate refusal to experience, these are what bring terrible expiation - the weeping and gnashing of teeth. From that He would have saved them if He could, but they would not. He never wept for Himself but He, knowing the Law, wept for the hard heartedness of Jerusalem, for He loved the place.

There is nothing more hurtful than to prepare a gift for the loved one and to have it cynically criticised and returned. If that is true of the individual gift it is equally true of the almoner's experience. To be the bearer of good things to the starving and needy and through false pride and bitterness to have them rejected is hard to bear. Jesus went through the personal and impersonal pain of rejection and His instant reaction was grief for those who rejected so blindly and arrogantly the marvellous opportunity for freedom He had incarnated to give them.

He never took pain to Himself therefore He never suffered from the illnesses that develop through mental suffering. He never made Himself the focal point. He stood on one side and made the Father the central figure. The Father was the expert; He had endowed the human form with divine energy, He alone could deal with the abuses, for He had instructed the Son to represent His attributes so as to destroy the illusions of the priests.

He did not demand blood sacrifices. He was not a relentless

avenging judge, He was the great giver, not the great demander. He was, in fact, the exact opposite of the human image. He was not an elderly gentleman who must not be crossed or disturbed who had a keen appetite, an eye for the first fruits and the tender kid and who could never be foxed as He always had one eye open and was a great stickler for etiquette. He was not a human priest depending on the richness of his robe to proclaim his greatness.

What a task Jesus undertook. The taking on of limitations in order to transcend them. He had to demonstrate that love was the serving of need instead of self-indulgence. He had to show that perfect love contains no fear. He had to live it to the glorious end. Live it until He could say to rational minded Thomas "If ye had known *me* Thomas, ye would have known my Father also, for I and my Father are one." That exciting oneness of mind and spirit the propagandists distorted into implying as a oneness of physical form, an absurdity which by the deft conjuring of words can be produced in any age and called blasphemy. There is either truth of thought and action, or the lack of it, and in any case the action decides the issue. If the works can be manifested, the formula must be correct. If, as Jesus said, they could not believe His words, then they must believe "for the very works' sake". That principle holds good in every profession, except that of the priest, who can still flourish on the letter of the law. The clerks, mechanics, craftsmen, services, doctors, architects and artists stand or fall by their works.

Jesus stressed the capacity of the individual to bring about the same oneness of spirit with Him as He enjoyed with His Father. He had to make God His Father real, by identifying Himself with Him. If you ask for anything, mention my Name; He will give it to you. We understand that perfectly in ordinary life. If anyone has the ear of authority and a favour is needed, that person is approached and asked if his name may be used to procure the favour more readily. His Father had given Him permission to be the mediator between these crassly ignorant creatures and Himself, so long as He sponsored their request. Jesus was to show them the limitations of their three dimensional existence and prove, by

Illusion

daily demonstration, that fearless love of humanity, selfless service and the continual focus of the mind on God are the start of fourth dimensional activities.

It was quite properly at a love feast that He was able to give His first demonstration. The body is the laboratory where every chemical transmutation takes place as routine work, and only fails to function when the various parts of the mechanism are neglected and out of order. It is not very difficult, in our generation, to understand that Christ was a scientist. He knew the capacity of His internal mechanism and knew also that to link it up to the great source of energy would, by direct contact, transform its substance, a very simple process. The factor for failure lay in the mind. If His mind took over the control, then it would be subject to the controversial mental wavelength radiating all around Him, and prudence, expediency, fear of results would have prevailed.

If only the illusionists could have understood His simplicity of motive and action, His warm-hearted, uncalculated givingness. Love is spontaneous combustion of opposite substance, God and man. Each one of the so-called miracles was a spontaneous flash of contact from the mind of the Father, through the body of the Christ, and out into the material substance, whether of human flesh, vegetable, animal, water or air. Jesus learnt through having a body, how the Father had planned the human race. He also learnt through His human experiences the limits of the human mind. According to those limits is the body reduced. He had to stress the limitless condition to which any human mind can attain. A child's mind linked to the eternal mind could demonstrate in action what the greatest mathematician might formulate as a proposition. The child demonstrating a universal law merely becomes a normal human being.

Jesus was also merely demonstrating how the human race could return to its state of normality. He never pretended that He was unique in any way or that the wonders He performed could never be done again. On the contrary, He came to raise matter to the limit of its original divine or harmonious condition. If He could do it, all could. Physically, He was the same as they were. Born into a working man's environment, with no privileges, but also no liabilities, He had to prove that ancestral heredity is an illusion. He did not depend only on His parents for His gifts or His blood.

There was a way by which all the past could be short-circuited. A man inherited himself. God held him responsible for his blood and for his talents. God was his Father; if he could recognise that fact, then all his weaknesses could be transmuted and changed and he could renew in his lifetime the vital energy that was his rightful inheritance. But he could not do that until he comprehended how vilely he was prostituting his opportunities. As long as he revelled in his excesses, then clearly he was not ready to admit his folly. But the Parent was ever there, ready to welcome him back, for fusion of hearts marks the return to normality.

By every means in His power Jesus endeavoured to find the simile or parable that would convey to the people the significance of the return of prodigal man to that new normality. In every case He stressed the capacity of the individual and the simplicity of the formula. Charity, the compassionate givingness from the heart is an essential factor in the Christian Initiation. To give is active; to receive is passive.

God is the giver, who created man in His image and endowed him with His own attributes, so that - with perseverance - man too should become divine. Until man becomes a giver, he is still separated from his divine capacity. Jesus knew that He was divine because He never separated Himself from His divine parent. He did not make it a personal, sensational achievement. He stated it as a cosmic fact and knew that it should be a universal experience.

It will be a universal experience when man has clarified for himself the distinction between personal experience and universal law. In Christ the cosmic law was made flesh, that is to say, the fourth dimensional activities latent in the blood were, through His personal experiences brought into normal expression. They were not acts of exhibitionism, but were a part of His normal self expression. That self or ego, consciously united in thought with the mind of God, expressed those thoughts in acts and demonstrated the simplicity of this new normality.

Illusion

Flesh and blood is composed of the elements, earth, air and water, it should have natural harmonies. The eternal life energy is Light. All matter contains a certain percentage of Life, but human substance has the greatest of all storage capacity. Through personal experience that life energy in the blood increases and decreases according to the mental processes of the individual. A Christ can receive the maximum, a fool the minimum, and by a fool I do not mean an idiot, but a foolish person who says in his heart "there is no God".

When the water supply is cut off at the main, one may turn the taps on, but only the water remaining in the pipes will flow and in time none will come through. That is the fate of the fool. He can live on his own mind until it dries up and then thrombosis, paralysis, arthritis, cancer, blindness, deafness, senile decay set in and he totters to his grave. Fourth dimensional man (or the Christian Initiate) can never totter to his grave. Once he starts on the return journey to his new normality the thrombosis will clear up and there will be no return, the incipient paralysis will change into a new activity, arthritis that slow crystallising of the blood by the critical mind, the hardening of the heart arteries through personal suffering, will slowly dissolve and become flexible. The cancer of repressed emotions will be eliminated out of the system, the blind shall see and the deaf hear and there will be no decay. The harmony of heavenly substance shall be standardised on earth and there shall be a new earth.

There was no senile decay in Christ. Fourth dimensional man can never be older than 33 in bodily functions and vigour. There is no age limit. One can start at 60 to end at 33. One learns the art of discarding from weakness, for His strength is made perfect through receiving human weakness. Christ took on the limitations of humanity to transcend them, not to manifest them. He had to manifest the normal, there is no condition of supernormal, the word "super" in connection with the normal is the prefix of ignorance. It is normal to function according to the various gifts and training of the individual each having different demonstrations of this normal activity. What is normal for an acrobat is not normal for a professor of economics; what was normal for Christ was not normal for the high priest. What was normal for Jesus at the age of 12 is not normal for an ordinary school boy.

We have to realise that Jesus was setting a new standard of normality and He would not be able to make the final demonstration until He was free in His own experience of the web of illusion that was being spun by tradition and fear through the minds of the enemies of spiritual progress. He could not be free until His body was free, "Whatsoever things are bound on earth are bound in Heaven." That is no gospel of "mind over matter" but the deifying of matter. Making matter divine is being able to take a human body back to the Creator, the Parent, and presenting that body in a perfect state to Him.

Jesus thus transcended all the old initiations. No initiate had perfected the body; no initiate had reconstructed, revitalised the form of God; none other had journeyed back again, conscious of every step of the way, leaving *the trail* and an invitation for re-union. The open-sesame to every door closed to strangers was the mention of His Name.

Chapter III.

PERSPECTIVE

Perspective is the relative value in time and space. It is the habit of the human mind to parcel out space and divide eternity into compartments of time. Thus we measure life in aeons and centuries, dynasties and decades, years and hours, and with our infinite capacity to separate the unities, we make of life a span, birth the portal, death the exit, the before and after unknowable.

Jesus started at the very beginning. The nature of His birth is mysterious from a three dimensional point of view. The choice of Mary to carry and protect the form of the great adventurer was not by chance, but was planned with great exactitude. Mary was the incarnation of selfless service. There were two great attributes she had to manifest, the perfect maternal love and utter normality. The truth concerning the conception was a secret imposed and kept by her with great faithfulness. The faithfulness and obedience earthed by Mary in her ordeal enabled Jesus to receive the perfect receptive faculty of the female from His mother; the positive male side of His nature He identified always with His divine parent, "My Father". Thus His illegitimacy was transformed from a stumbling block to a foundation stone.

In the love of Mary the mother there was no possessiveness, no clutch on the son, no sentimentality. Her body was a chosen vehicle, she gave it gladly, but with no heroics. In her we have love and wisdom perfectly blended. She is the model for all women to emulate. She had no self love therefore she was chosen as a vehicle to give birth to Love. She was not afraid of her primitive surroundings and because she was unresisting there was no mental disturbance, no emotional disharmony. Mary, the unpossessive mother, becomes the universal pattern of normal motherhood.

Christ incarnated as a man to co-ordinate and harmonise in His body the opposite sex energies, the receptivity of the female and the positive expression of the male. The balance of the energy in His blood is fourth dimensional. The desire to heal and comfort and bring forth a living form is the urge of the female. When you have a balanced mind, receptive to inspiration and positive in expression you have a great man, capable of great deeds. When you have a selfless receptive with fearless positive expression in action, you have a great woman capable of great deeds.

Surplus positive energy shuts off receptivity; surplus receptive energy shuts off positive expression and produces the psychic medium. Christ was a conscious medium, consciously transmitting co-ordinated energy. Mary was a conscious receptive with a fearless positive expression, the greatest of all women of her time and probably of all times. She treasured all things concerning her little son in her heart and in that she was wise. In the heart is no self love, no possessive clutch, no fear. The mind is Judas, the betrayer of love. The heart is Mary, the treasurer of love. Christ is the body, the co-ordinator of the heart and brain, the transmitter of Love. The Father God is the source. Can the human race today get the perspective in time and space of that great scientific achievement of Mary and Jesus, two thousand years ago? If it does, then the second manifestation of Love in fifth dimensional activity is an imminent certainty.

In the energy of Love there is no repetitive action. That is why the Father was able to inform the world through the agency of His Son, "Behold! I make all things new." The human mind has no conception of newness. It knows how to make new things old, and how to repair old things to have the appearance of a new article. But to create something absolutely new is beyond the conception of the third dimensional mind which only knows its own limits. There is a limit to mathematical calculations, but no limit to spontaneous combustion.

Christ never healed the same disease in exactly the same way. No two men are exactly alike, universally similar, individually they differ. It is essential that Christ who incarnated to serve the needs of the human race should demonstrate in action how the Law of Love energy worked

Perspective

through the human instrument. To get a perfect result it must work spontaneously. To achieve spontaneous action there must be co-ordination between the source, the instrument and the object. When the instrument consciously connects to the source, the code word being "Father," then the instrument and the source are connected. The instrument then focuses on the object. The minus condition of leprosy or blindness is transmitted straight to the source, a flash of contact and perfect atomic energy is injected - the object is cured.

Can the scientist of today explain in simple words to the ordinary man how to split the atom? Would they hand over their £500,000,000 laboratory to the general public to marufacture eternal energy for their own use, free and unrestricted? Two thousand years ago Jesus was offering eternal energy to anyone public minded enough to accept the training. One physician, one civil servant and some fishermen formed the nucleus and by degrees others were attracted. It could never attract a large public because there was no apparent lure of personal power. Service for service sake has no attraction then or now, but there was a fascination about the talk of eternal energy, there might be something in it. Quacks always have an appeal to the imaginative mind but are an anathema to the orthodox. Here was a person who talked like a quack but acted like a superman. He did things that others could not do, even the high priest himself could not do the works that this man Jesus did. He was no stickler for the letter of the law. He healed on the Sabbath, ate what He liked, when He liked and was publicly revealing secret knowledge, educating or corrupting according to the point of view, so that all and sundry should benefit from this cosmic energy. "Ask and ye shall receive." "Ye have not because ye ask not." That giving away of secret contact and making universal direct access to the Source made Him a menace to the big mystery combines and He had to be eliminated. From the moment that Jesus publicised the formula for universal receptivity of eternal energy, vested interests sought to destroy Him. If they had not known that atomic energy could be received by direct contact of the individual with the Godhead, they would have let Jesus alone, as He scrupulously observed the Roman occupational regulations. But because He could put into operation what they only enunciated, they were the letter - He *was* the Law, for that superiority they insisted on the death sentence.

By the time He was ready for the final demonstration of the truth, that there is no death in atomic energy. In Gethsemane He was shown the pattern of resurrection. He had to prove that atomic is greater than mental energy. The mind can order the destruction of the body but the heart action is greater than the brain action since there is more blood in the heart than in the brain. If the brain is surrendered to the Distributor of cosmic energy the mental wavelength has no power to cancel the blood radiation. Jesus surrendered cerebral activity to the Father who was able to inject into the obedient Son atomic energy sufficient to reconstruct the physical organic structure. The law of eternal energy was thus earthed for all time in flesh and blood.

The part that Judas played in this cosmic drama is that of the villain, the base betrayer of the hero into the power of the enemy. Yet Judas merely acted as any reasonable man of the world would act under similar circumstances. I stress the word "reasonable," for undoubtedly he reasoned out the situation. He had been associated with Jesus for some time; he was one of the trusted comrades and he had witnessed the many amazing acts of compassion performed by Jesus on strangers and sceptics. Judas had a business mind and could not comprehend how anyone gifted as Jesus undoubtedly was and acknowledging His divine origin did not impose His will on the people.

Judas had a great respect for power and authority and if Jesus had followed Lucifer's advice and given an exhibition of how eternal life energy worked through the human instrument, if only he had turned super-showman and forced the people to acknowledge His greatness, Judas would have been His right hand man and His advertising manager. Judas lived in his mind and the wisdom of the heart was a closed book to him.

Lucifer is master of the mental wavelength and through the brain recruits his instruments, through them he dictates, through them he wields

Perspective

vicarious world power. The brain without the heart is the strength of Lucifer; the co-ordinating of the heart with the brain is the strength of Christ. The heart is the co-ordinating organ, the brain is the sifter, the separator. Analysis, criticism, comparisons are cerebral functions; emotion is generated through the thought processes. In the average person the brain governs the heart action and the body must respond to the cerebral energy. Therefore if the mind is dominated by Luciferian agents and supreme power be the bribe, we can easily understand the boring repetition of catastrophic events brought about by the lust for power. Lucifer is lust; Christ is Love. "The Prince of this world cometh who hath no part in me." He knew then; we know now.

Where then lies the sin of Judas? Is it a sin to be a business man? Is it a sin to have a reasonable mind? It is a sin not to use opportunities; it is a sin to be ignorant when one has the capacity learn. It is a sin to love oneself and to exploit one's neighbour. It is a sin to commercialise Love. It is a sin to be a business man first and a follower of Christ last. And then again, what is sin? Original sin is fear.

The record of the fall of man from his divine status of harmony was brought about by the female receptive tapping the earth station, fascinated by the mental stimulus, shutting off the longwave station and thereby cutting off communication from celestial G.H.Q. The result of that flagrant disobedience was fear and walking and talking with God was no longer part of the natural function of man. It was at that period of the human race that it lost is fourth and fifth dimensional activity. The human mechanism still retains its original design and Christ's mission was to earth the energy and put the self-starter, as it were, again into operation.

Judas had the same capacity as Peter or John to renew the contact with the Father through the example of the Son. Lucifer had designs on all of them and Jesus told Peter of it, but Peter was a warm-hearted man and his love for Jesus was of the heart. Judas was cold and calculating and love cannot be imposed on the mind. Jesus never appealed to the emotions of His followers. Love as He lived it was the serving of need.

The need of the friend, the stranger, the enemy was all the same to Him. He could not refuse to supply their need. Love has not power to refuse or withhold. When the mind does not compare, when it never makes the ego the focal point of its activity, then it becomes aware only of human need, then the individual realises that Love and the attributes of love are not virtues but the effortless functioning of the heart.

The mind of Judas betrayed Christ as it betrayed love in all the ages; the domination of the mind over matter is the great betrayal embodied in Judas. The surrender of the mind and the domination of the heart is the supreme scientific achievement of all times, embodied in Jesus. There are two opposite conditions, good and evil, fulfilling the law or breaking the law. If one fulfils the law one becomes a Christ and is no longer subject to it. If one breaks the law one becomes vulnerable to all the penalties incurred. Mankind has very imperfect knowledge of the working of the Law of Love. We are quite aware that we do not love God and find it very difficult to love our particular neighbours. When we become aware that the word "neighbour" includes all relatives and all nationalities, then the task seems farcical and we fall back on the comfort afforded by the so-called higher critics of the Bible and feel that at worst it is falsely translated and at best was probably not uttered at all. Unfortunately that does not exclude us from suffering the penalty exacted from the ignorant.

Designed to receive revelation, we are not excused for not receiving it. We are not saved from catastrophe by not knowing how natural laws function. We drown; we burn; we freeze. Nature does not act emotionally. Why do we think that God does? Why should an individual be excused from the results of working havoc in the world on the grounds of not knowing what he was doing when he has the capacity for knowing? Every human being will be judged on a capacity standard and ignorance will be no plea for mercy, but a condition of utter shame. "Ye have not because ye ask not." Is there any man, woman or child who has never learnt to ask for what it wants? To know the letter and not to become the law was no justification two thousand years ago and will

Perspective

certainly be no justification now.

Jesus always appealed to capacity, was always trying to stimulate the average mind to an understanding of the simplicity of the new method of approach. He knew the danger of the subtle minds opposing Him. The antidote to subtlety is simplicity; to secrecy is publicity; to accusation is silence. If we want to know how the Law of Love functions we can study the life of Jesus. He was the law made flesh. We have no excuse for ignorance. Let us also face the fact of our own capacity and do not let us sidetrack our minds to consider the ignorance of others or assume that they have never had any chance to correct it. We cannot judge the mind from the outside. No individual knows the inner working of another person's mind and we can never judge our neighbour. It is ourselves we have to account for, not them. Talent and capacity, actions and inertia, we shall have to unpack our character on the other side at the 'great customs house', have the results of our earthly visit checked and scrutinised. We took so much with us of capacity on our journey, in what condition of experience do we return? On that depends our future destination. We cannot travel further than our love of humanity will take us - will it be to the suburbs or will it be to the celestial City itself? "I go to prepare a place for you for where I am there shall ye be also." Jesus was the only one who knew the way back, in whose memory all experience was alive. He knew that these faithful friends of His would be able to travel on His love energy straight to where He would be, so He impressed this fact on them. The law of attraction operates in both worlds and is a cosmic condition, the brain to receive the direction, the heart to operate the energy. Could anything be more simple? A child could work it, in fact a child would find it easier than a professional.

Chapter IV.

DISTINCTION

The only certainties of life are those gained through experience. Daily experience of the elements teaches us the effect of water, whether rain, river or sea, also that fire burns. Through different sensations we develop our capacity for discernment and become able to distinguish lust from love; falsehood from truth; selfishness from unselfishness. Everybody's problems are different; universally they are the same, but individually they differ in degree. What use at the end of life to realise the follies of youth? Jesus incarnated to save youth from folly, to provide a way of escape from muddle-mindedness, to demonstrate a universal method of contact to enable youth to receive daily directions for the daily path. "Give us this day our daily bread." Jesus could never have achieved His fourth dimensional power if He had not made daily contact with the Father. A house dependent on electricity for cooking, heating and lighting knows the deprivation if the supply is cut off for a day. If Jesus had forgotten the Father, even for a day, the immensity of His task would have depressed Him and self-pity would have flooded His being. The ingratitude of the people, the stupidity of His associates, the intolerable loneliness of His personal life could have submerged His mission. He would have done His best, the Father could not expect more.

Such thoughts have no power of entry into the trained mind kept in constant contact. Lucifer can get no answer if the mind is engaged on its own private line with God. If one is not ringing up, one can be rung up. That is the first distinction we can make to ensure our certainty for true direction. If our mind is engaged in contacting the mind of Christ, if we establish a minute to minute service with Him then we achieve an absolute certainty of direction, we do not wonder, we know. Jesus did not wonder if it was really the Father doing the works, He knew. It was because He asserted His knowledge that He so exasperated the priests. It was their prerogative to dispense knowledge.

Distinction

It is still thought by many today that doubt is a more becoming attitude of mind than certainty. Therefore it is not surprising that governments all over the world depend on individual brains to solve world problems. They study the past and from the past forecast the future. Can anything be more abysmally ignorant if the true object is to progress?

How can we, by looking back, press forward? We have been goose-stepping for 2,000 years and are still marching round the barrack square. The news of the atomic bomb brings us to a halt and at this moment we are standing to attention, suddenly arrested from our repetitive movements.

Most people are horrified at the appalling opportunity for destruction that man's mind has devised. It is dimly sensed that what can destroy might also create, and in creation there is no fear. Fear comes through splitting the atom, but in the unity of the atom there is no fear. In the action of separation the exposure of the unknown magnitude of the released energy causes fear in the third dimensional mind of man.

In Christ there was no fear. There was obedience and wisdom. The Father knew that only in service could man come safely into his fourth dimensional inheritance. Somehow He must make the distinction clear to ensure safe transmission. There was only one fool-proof way, through Love to power. That is where Lucifer and Christ divided; Lucifer to split the world and Jesus to unite the world. Lucifer's objective is to deify the brain and Christ's is to make all human substance divine. Lucifer's banner is power, the development of the ego into superman, the domination of matter by the mind, the exploitation of the neighbour for the elevation of the ego. Secrecy, mystery, exclusiveness, darkness and fear are the outward and visible signs of Luciferian strategy.

We must remember that Lucifer and Christ are working for the same object, namely world domination. Lucifer, if he wins, will become world dictator: Christ, if He wins will become world saviour. Lucifer works through mass movements, Christ through minorities. One free man can release innumerable prisoners. Thousands herded in bondage are helpless and Lucifer's secret weapon is fear.

The contest between these two great protagonists has always been equal and the result unpredictable for the free will of the individual is the deciding factor. The hour of total victory "No man knoweth - not even the Son, save the Father only." There can be no second coming of Love's manifestation if Lucifer wins. If world destruction is accomplished, then Lucifer has the world to himself. How much does it matter Mr. Cynic if you and I are not here to be incommoded by it?

Why did the world matter to Jesus? Why did He think it worth saving? It meant personal sweat and blood, it meant giving all and getting nothing. It was not reasonable. No. It was a divine conception, divinely executed. The prince of the world competition and the Prince of Peace are both accoutred for the fray in the armour of their own certainties, fear and Love. "My peace I give unto you, NOT as the world giveth give I unto you." "Ye have not because ye ask not." How can one distinguish between Lucifer and Christ, between expediency and certainty, imagination and direction? How can anyone discern the difference between desire and need, wishful thinking and inspiration? How can an apparently negative point of view bring positive results? The incarnation and resurrection are meaningless unless the universal law embodied in Jesus becomes individual experience; so that love, peace of mind and body, certainty of action and daily inspiration bring the discernment of mind.

A receptive mind reacts in positive efficiency. A positive mind has a limited activity. A receptive mind has limitless transmission. A receptive mind is capable of inspiration; a positive mind is closed to fourth dimensional knowledge and is afraid. The moment the mind registers fear, it contacts Lucifer. When youth puts service before self, it starts on the modern Pilgrim's Progress, the path that leads to freedom and fulfilment.

The mind controls the senses and an uncontrolled mind acts in a licentious way. The human mind cannot control nature's laws. It cannot stop the storm or control volcanic eruptions. It cannot entirely control the human functions, it has no power to control the receptivity of the blood

Distinction

and cause it to refuse a disease germ, nor can it prevent the transmission of that germ. It has its limits, so youth is educated in order to learn its own limits, not to comprehend its capacity. Limit is Lucifer's trademark. "Capacity," Christ's clarion call. "They that have ears to hear," let them hear that call to fearless experience.

What is the difference between self-expression and self-indulgence? What part does passion play in the life of the Christian Initiate? It is said that it is no use looking to Christ's life to solve the problem as nothing is recorded of any personal experience. Jesus was concerned in demonstrating universal law through an individual instrument, therefore to imitate His personal life and to enforce celibacy because he never married is obviously to misinterpret the letter or pattern of the Law. Passion is that substance of life energy that holds the seeds of creative activity; the union of receptive and positive currents creates form and substance and was designed so to do. It is a cosmic harmony and as such should be a consummation of ecstasy. Jesus was the Law; He could not break it. There was no woman, save Mary, whose mind and body were in harmony with Love. Passion is generated through cerebral activity particularly through the eyes, sight and touch. Through the senses men demonstrate their dimensional status. Third dimensional man is a taker, a possessor, a withholder. Jesus, the first perfect fourth dimensional man, was a giver: He possessed nothing, He withheld nothing. There is our example. We cannot imitate Him, we can only follow in His footsteps, and through our own individual experience, attain our own freedom.

Chapter V.

BEFORE AND AFTER

"Before Abraham was, I AM," said Jesus and He constantly referred to His intimacy with the Father as having been established a long time before His birth. His memory of pre-natal events, His sense of continuity and His prediction of His return journey were all part of the pattern of eternal life. He succeeded in making His disciples understand that there was a before birth and after death existence, and that supreme importance was to be attached to the opportunities given and taken by the individual during his lifetime. A life devoted to self-expression and self-indulgence placed the individual in very uncomfortable circumstances as Dives found. Those who denied themselves to themselves in this life found freedom in after conditions, but one had to earn that freedom on earth.

Worldly experience is vital. Until we have individually become the Law of Love on earth, we are not free. We must return again and again until passion is transmuted into compassion and possessiveness into freedom. Jesus had to live the life He did to prove that passion can be transmuted into compassion and that in His love for humanity there was not personal clutch. His disciples were free "to walk with Him no more" when they found His sayings too difficult and unpalatable. If His love could not attract them back then they must go. But they found that they could never leave Him, not even Judas.

Poor Judas thought he knew better but found that life without that magnetic personality was not to be borne and so he made that last and final gesture of pitiful ignorance. He took his own life and thus bound himself on the wheel of life that turns and turns with the same monotonous rhythm of recurrence in time. Jesus came to reconstruct the wheel of life into the spiral of ascension. Before Christ's advent there was no escape from karma. "An eye for an eye and a tooth for a tooth" is the karmic law which means that what you do to your neighbour in one life is done by

Before and After

your neighbour to you in another incarnation. If you have tortured him in unenlightened days, then in some life he reappears possibly as a surgeon, a soldier or a motorist and your body receives the pain you have caused to be inflicted on your neighbour.

It is essentially just, it operates inexorably, unemotionally and we call it fate. We cannot escape our destiny, we have made it ourselves. If we take our own life because we find our condition beyond endurance then when we incarnate again, we pick up our humanity as we left it and have a far harder task than before. We start life with a suicidal tendency, with an introvert mind, ourselves again the focal point. Only by learning to tune in to the mind of Christ, He who never on earth put Himself first, can we change the current of our self-centredness and then our freedom begins.

It is the same with all human weakness - drink, drugs, cerebral instability, depravity. Medical science can alleviate, can with co-operation sometimes cure, but can never promise that there will be no recurrence. Only Jesus who knew human nature and the reactions of the mind on the body, could promise an immediate and final cure, by blood transfusion. His blood was class "A", no finer or purer blood had ever circulated in a body. He knew the power of blood. He never ceased to talk about it. He never ceased to demonstrate it. In His blood was atomic energy, a spark cured all diseases.

The life energy in the blood is eternally recording life's activities, therefore no man can ever get away from himself. Before birth and after death is the I Am of every individual. The world brings the ego into visibility; it takes on the substance of its environment; it becomes a human being. The record of all its previous existence is in its blood energy and though third dimensional man cannot remember in detail, his conscience is a constant reminder of past experience and warns against repetition.

Conscience is the outer casing of memory. In some people the blood is more magnetic, places and people seem familiar and the finer radiations of memory stir and consciousness begins to function. Other people assert that they are not pscyhic and never have had any experiences that could ever make them believe in reincarnation. They are afraid of it for it would not suit Lucifer for people to remember and never be foolish again. Positive self-assertive limited minds are necessary to him; the longer he can keep them ignorant the greater the chance of world destruction, "Eat, drink and be merry for tomorrow we die," is the motto for fools. Give to eat, give to drink, for today we live and life is eternal is the wise man's axiom.

Whether we believe it or not, reincarnation is a fact that marks the boundary between the third and fourth dimensional activity. When we achieve our Christhood, we shall be free of the bondage of the world. Reincarnation is bondage, we are bound by the shackles of our disobedience. Hate is a shackle; fear is another; pride is another. Where we hate we must learn to serve. What we fear we must learn to pity. Pride is self-esteem, in love there is no self-esteem.

We alone can decide how many lives it will take us to get our freedom. That it can be done in a lifetime, Jesus came to prove. He put no limits for it does not matter to God. A thousand years, a single day it is all the same to Him. It is our fate, not His; ours is the choice. If He could have moved in the matter, if it depended on Him, the miracle would have happened aeons ago. If He could change us arbitrarily it would have been done. Obviously then the whole responsibility lies on us.

Jesus said, "Of myself I can do nothing, it is the Father that doeth the works," thus He took away the burden of responsibility substituting a new idea, that of co-operation. It was a bombshell to orthodoxy, an anathema to priestly authority. If it had been understood, if co-operation had been put into daily use and daily manifestation there could not have materialised the different aspects of comprehension embodied in the structural Christian edifices of today.

When Christ ascended He could not have envisaged the period that would elapse before the letter would again become the Law. He *knew* that it was not a matter of time; His fourth dimensional mind was not bound by time but was time. Past, present and future were co-ordinated

Before and After

in Him. The past fused into the present, the future became a mental illusion, for God is, love is, life is the *same*, yesterday, today and for ever. Distance is eliminated and "The kingdom of God," He said, "is within you." You cannot travel away from Love. The Father is only a flash away, you cannot measure a flash of light in time or space.

Gradually He brought the unity into focus and time was reduced to a day. In a day is all opportunity, in a flash is the miracle. In time is indefinite delay. He had to try to teach those minds, corroded with centuries of the hoarded past, that *now* is the accepted time, *now* is the moment of salvation. He and the Father could only work in the spark of the moment, for one could not create life by contemplation.

Time was eternal sparking and every spark was time. The life energy in the blood is Light. God the Father is the source of Light, is the quickener. When the entity has received all it can receive, it is quickened and is able to move and function, and according to its past experience will it be able to receive much or little. It will choose the parents who have similar past experiences so that the blood will correspond in substance with the detail of experience. The individual who dies a drunkard must incarnate in parents who have or had uncontrolled desire in their past or present experience. A still born child provides for the parents, one or both, the expiation for a past offence against a defenceless infant. There is no infringement of the law of expiation, an eye for an eye, a life for a life.

When the individual becomes conscious of its capacity to finish with the breaking of the law and has the desire to love instead of hate, to create instead of to destroy, then comes that moment of decision and the soul announces the fact. "I will arise and go to my Father and will say unto Him, 'Father I have sinned . . . and am no more worthy to be called Thy son'." Instantly the reconciliation of opposites is accomplished.

It is necessary to understand that God never changes, His will is Law, His will is Love. God is Love. He sent Jesus into the world to teach the world how the Law of Love functions. Christ loved humanity. From the grammatical point of view, God is the noun; Christ is the verb. Their relationship is a harmony, their identities distinct. A representative of a firm is not the firm; a journalist represents his paper abroad, but must not be mistaken for the newspaper itself. Jesus represented the Father God on earth, but was *not* God the Father. He is the faithful ambassador, eloquently demonstrating with perfect personal integrity, the object of His mission entrusted to Him by His King. How could He convey to the human mind, infinitely variable, unstable and fluctuating, the unchanging quality of Love? How make them understand that flesh and blood in their original conception were divine, vibrant, luminous, exquisite in form and substance? By writing? By contemplation? Those were the old methods, there must be something new, so incarnation, resurrection and ascension provided a new consciousness, a new capacity for experience.

It is not really difficult to understand that Christ could not write His own autobiography. He had to live the written word and If He wrote on parchment, it would perish; if He wrote it in blood, if He became the Word, then the word could never perish, it must live. The blood of Jesus lives today for He had in His veins atomic energy, drawn from the living, unchanging substance of the body of God, from whom the whole human race has drawn its infinite energy. The blood of the average individual is so adulterated with fear that there is very little of the pure essence of life in them. There is just enough to keep the blood circulating, the muscles moving and lungs working; often not enough to keep the body in the minimum state of of health for the space of a lifetime.

If God is the same yesterday, today and for ever, man is exactly the reverse. He is lacking in the substance that makes God unchangeable, namely Love. God lacks the substance that makes man unstable, namely fear. How then can man return to his divine, pre-Adamic state? Fear was earthed through disobedience. Love was earthed again through obedience. The Naaman type of mind rejects this as being much too simple; he wants something more complicated, more exclusive and also rather more showy.

The river Jordan held no special substance for the curing of leprosy, but somehow Naaman had to lose his pride and how could that

Before and After

be accomplished? It was the barrier between him and freedom. It was his karmic inheritance. Only by voluntarily losing self- consciousness could it be done. The prophet was inspired. He gave Naaman the means, the choice was his, either to keep his pride and his disease, or relinquish his pride and the disease would leave him.

Disobedience is not only a mental condition, it is the gold mine of the medical profession. Every classic and obscure disease is traceable to inherited fear and provides the disharmony of mankind with nature and of man with mankind. The life of the air, earth and water are either in harmony or disharmony with the individual constitution and will either invigorate or poison. There is a whole octave of nervous diseases caused by mental strain, insanity and deformity. The individual inherits himself, bringing his own insulation from the love energy into visibility at birth. It takes different expressions and will respond to different treatments. Everyone has the environment that will give the maximum opportunity of release from the bondage imposed by the ego's own ignorance of cosmic law. The most common of all barriers erected in self-defence against any unpalatable knowledge of fact, is the endowing of God with an erratic, incomprehensible and sinister personality, with a personal grudge against the individual. Alternatively God is banished into remotest space and becomes abstract, incomprehensible, a sound, a word, an oath.

Is it strange that human beings thus insulated from truth gain very little knowledge life after life wherewith to fashion a better body, more aware of its potential divine capacity? If it had not been for organised religion, the Nazi principles would have enslaved the world. Between escaping world enslavement and achieving the freedom of divine heredity is a great gap of inexperience. Good will is not enough. Good intentions may never materialise. We all need a new experience, a new consciousness, a rebirth. It was the problem of Nicodemus. How can a man be born again? Why was Jesus demanding the impossible, or seemed to be. Scientists of the day have to coin words to explain new works. Jesus could only use the words people understood to indicate a new experience. How explain the fourth dimension as a living experience, a new and living way to men who only believed in what they could see and touch? How describe rebirth when they knew not the law of birth and accepted death?

Words cannot convey freedom to the incarcerated, they are a mockery. So to all people to whom words are of primary importance, rebirth must be the delusion of an idealist. To the Christian Initiate it is a real experience. When I say, real, I write as a true materialist. Jesus lived the life of a materialist in its true sense. He was the truth, the way to truth. He was life. He had made His soul body, composed of eternal energy, harmonise with His physical body. The outer protective casing is designed to enable the soul body to live in harmony with all created substance.

Jesus could walk on water, if the need was there. He could disappear out of their sight, if it was His need to do so. Fourth dimensional activities only operate when set in motion by the need of the individual or his neighbour. They cannot function on personal desire energy, however strong that desire may be. Therefore Jesus was unable to demonstrate rebirth in a single act. He was the expression of it. He had unconditionally surrendered His life to the Father.

Jesus had changed the capacity of the average Jew from accumulator to distributor. If only the Jews of His day had understood why He incarnated into their race, the whole history of the world would have been different. The Jewish blood is the most receptive of all racial blood; it draws to itself the most valued of earth's substances, gold and precious stones. It is collective by instinct and activity. It has the capacity to inherit the earth. If Jesus could have exhibited outside the power that operated inside, the Jews could have understood. But they were asked to accept a king whose royal robes were blazing with unseen jewels. His soul body was the most glorious that has ever incarnated. But they could not discern it; they could not handle His jewels or finger His golden glory. What use to them was a king with no commercial value? Away with Him.

He asked of them unconditional surrender of commercial

Before and After

ambition as the first principle of life. "Seek ye FIRST the kingdom of God and His righteousness and all these things will be added unto you." Jesus always spoke in terms of law. He never said, "perhaps", or "if you are good", but uncompromisingly He always insisted on action. "Seek." All His life He had to search for human sparks, and searching found a few. He found Peter, Matthew, John; and through them, others were attracted. The Jews refused to spark; fear of reprisals from Jehovah, deterred them and the priestly gestapo would be on their tracks. Fear. Again and again Jesus said, "Fear not," "Come unto me." There was authority in His voice, in His works, but no outside badge to reassure them. Yet it was their blood He had in His veins. Their blood which He had to purge from fear. Their blood He took back to the Father. Their blood that holds the key to liberate their race. Their king who waits for recognition and who cannot come again until their hearts attract Him earthwards. It was their city over which He wept, knowing in His consciousness the tears that Jews must shed in towns all over the world because they refused to give their king the freedom of their city. No wonder He insisted that they must be born again, to die consciously to third dimensional possessiveness and be born free on the next spiral of experience to become the givers of the human race.

Rebirth is the conscious acceptance of the individual of a new mind and a new body, with no private reservation. Jesus undertook the training if any would offer voluntarily to undergo it. It is a training and because the quick Jewish mind could not see any personal advantage to be gained by undergoing it, Jesus then offered it to every man. Necessarily those that had least to lose started first; those like Himself, despised and judged by outside appearances. It is hard to imagine the state of this world if Jew and Gentile had entirely refused - almost as hard as to imagine the state of the world tomorrow if the Jews accepted Him today.

Chapter VI.

TODAY

"Today" is a fascinating description of time - the common denominator of all human experience. Something happens to somebody every day. On a certain day rebirth was a happening in the life of Paul of Tarsus, a completely new experience for his mind was changed, and through that change his feet were set on a diametrically opposite path to the one he had been travelling the day before. A *volte face* of world significance. From life to life he had been preparing his body for this very experience and when it came it was almost too much for him. The flash of contact nearly killed him, for atomic energy meeting a resisting substance causes death. In Paul's case this flesh took the charge of life, but it rendered him unconscious.

It must be remembered that at the resurrection Christ had made His body into a transformer so that the average man could, by tuning in his life energy to that of the Christ's body, be relayed by Him to the direct source of life, the Father. "No man cometh unto the Father save through me." Again a simple direction for safe transmission that has been ignored.

Life after life we are preparing our bodies to take the voltage of energy that Paul of Tarsus received from the ascended invisible body of the Christ, Jesus. Before the resurrection, Jesus was preparing His body to take the full charge of eternal energy for the reconstruction of the atoms of His flesh and blood. At the resurrection, in the privacy of the tomb prepared for Him and sealed by the authorities, the happening took place and fourth dimensional interpenetration of material substance was perfected. Once again flesh and blood were rendered divine, in harmony with the Source. The actual time of the occurrence must have been a flash; the time of preparation 33 years. The period of preparation differs in lives, owing to the free will of the ego. The happenings must always be a flash on whatever day the body is receptive enough to receive the charge. It can only come to mankind from the Christ body.

Today

The preparation for Jesus was the increasing of His receptivity until He could stand the proximity of the Father and not die. If His resurrection body could not have taken the charge, He could not have ascended, nor could He have broadcast to His disciples of His safe arrival. The preparation of the individual is to become receptive enough to stand the proximity of the Christ.

It was essential that the world should understand the science of reconstruction, therefore He sent the disciples to the remote parts of the world to earth the energy through the soles of their feet and to instruct the minds of the people how to focus. Minds, heart and feet. The mind must focus; the inner eye (or pineal gland) should receive the pattern, the heart to control, the blood to transmit, and the feet to earth the energy. The disciples carried their whole equipment with them; and to teach them confidence in His power to supply their need, they were to take the minimum of luggage on their mission. There was no other way for them to learn. They must establish confidence as a substance of their being. They could do no miracles without learning that through them all things could be done by Christ, and without that contact things would go wrong.

There are many people like Paul of Tarsus who glory in difficulties, but the effortless functioning of Christ is by far the most perfect method. Paul demonstrates the fight and Christ the surrender. The more sweat and bloodshed, the greater appears the human sacrifice, but also the greater recoil of human beings from Christian effort. Fourth dimensional activity is effortless, it is a happening, an ecstasy of freedom from strife. If the ego does not fight the ego, there is no sweat, no blood. Agony of mind is crucifixion. Focus of the mind on the risen Christ is prelude to resurrection.

The mission of the disciples was to tell the world of the fact of the new and living experience, and Paul, with the hot enthusiasm of the convert, focused the minds of the people on the personal aspect. People all over the world are interested in personal experience and are apt to miss the universal law that lies behind all individual experience. Christ was the voluntary victim of man's ignorance. Paul, the karmic prisoner of self-induced bondage, recognised that the one way of escape for all men of all nationalities, all mentalities, all social classes, all displaced persons, was to have the mind of Jesus. To that end he strove with great integrity to learn how to love. He did not realise that to tune in to Love is to *become* love; to tune into wisdom is to *be* wise.

In the surrender of all mental conflict, Jesus identified Himself with the Father and became one with Him. This flashing of mind to mind holds the maximum of exhilaration. Man lives life after life of ignorance, striving in the darkness for illumination, employing strange means of mortification of the body to attain a mental contact. One flash of contact with the mind of Christ and knowledge *is* revealed. He tried to teach men how to receive knowledge, for revelation cannot be induced. The process of resurrection was pure revelation flashed into a mind trained for 33 years to receive it. That training was to turn the Jewish mind from contemplating and living in the past into becoming the embodiment of the present.

The mind of Jesus became the model instrument to which all minds tuning in would also operate on the same wavelength and would thus have the same physical reactions. Paul of Tarsus knew that if he could have Christ's mind, he would have Christ's body, the two were one. His own mind had produced his own body and he wanted to change both, that they might become "like unto His glorious body". He knew the pattern, but how was he to achieve the substance? As far as humanly possible, Paul strove to tune in to Christ, sought to identify himself with Him. His very self-consciousness was the greatest barrier. When one identifies oneself with oneself, however well intentioned, however humbly, one is still limited by that thought of self. When the Father functioned through Jesus, the reaction of the son was thanks: "Father, I thank Thee that *Thou*" — not, "Father, I thank Thee that I." He never mistook His channelhood for personal effort.

We may be fascinated by the personal experiences of the disciples, but it must never be to them that we turn to understand the incomprehensible, it must always be to the mind of Christ who alone can reveal the truth to us. The human body is the instrument designed and created to receive and transmit all cosmic energy. Television, wireless, radio-location are part of fourth dimensional man's normal service. When his senses are fully developed, when his eyes see, his ears hear, when his fingertips can touch time, when his feet can replenish the earth, then eternity becomes the sparking moment, the moment is eternity. Perfect man has no past and is not separated from his future. He is as God, who is Love. If man were never separated from Love, there would be no division in time. Thus eternity becomes Love in activity.

Mental pain is conscious separation from Love; physical pain is the reaction on the body of that separation. Love is Light. Jesus was the Light of the world. His blood was radio-active. His blood sparked harmony; our blood sparks disharmony in various contagious diseases. The blood is always transmitting the substance of which it is composed. Therefore it was not a virtue but a new normality that Jesus was earthing for the human race. No man can keep his blood to himself, there would be no epidemics if he could.

Jesus came to teach how the only certain cure for all ailments was blood transfusion, but He insisted that there was only one pure source from which to draw and that was direct from the Father, God. He drew it direct, therefore His blood would save the world from death and disease. Sceptics may blink at the experiment of raising Lazarus from his decayed condition, but re-animating matter when you have in your veins the required antidote to death is not a miracle, it is a natural law. The miracle was that Jesus had so perfected His mind and body that there was no resistance to the inflow of eternal energy. He was able to transmit what He received unadulterated by personal emotion. Self-pity never insulated, desire never corroded and selfishness never hardened His arteries.

Jesus never exhibited pride in His achievements. For Him the world was divided into two classes, not the good and the bad, but the wise and the foolish, the wheat and the tares with the harvest of separation. The parable of the wise and the foolish virgins is most poignantly told. How great was their folly in letting their lamps go out because they could not believe that the bridegroom would ever come in their lifetime; their futile effort to borrow experience showed the immutability of the law in unemotional operation, shutting them out from the marriage feast.

Jesus vividly describes the working of this Law of Love. Die to yourself and you live for ever; live to yourself and you die. In parable and example He strove to impress on them the folly of ignorance. Beggar or millionaire had equal chances to receive the riches He could transmit to them. Harlot or high priest could receive forgiveness for past ignorance and become the children of Light. In the Father God was no distinction of personal transgression. The reaction of ignorance returned inevitably to the source, sin to the sinner and love to the lover.

How then does forgiveness operate? It is like a junction where travellers can alight and transfer from a train going in one direction to a train bound for a different destination. Jesus became that junction. Travellers on the Lucifer line could halt at the 'Forgiveness Junction', if they could recognise it in time. The Father endowed Jesus with the power to forgive sin on earth. He knew the searching quality of this inter-penetrating light. It exposed to the sinner the quality of his mental processes; it stripped him of illusion, it threw a beam across his path showing the quality of the road on which he was travelling. The light revealed what the darkness hid. At this junction of the cross roads, Jesus stands, not as a judge, but as a comrade, with hand outstretched to help the wayfarer over that delicate and difficult patch of ground when he voluntarily acknowledges that he is on the wrong road and wants to change over. He, who surrendered pride, has earned the right to say, "Come."

To understand the Christian Initiation, one must first of all understand the personality of Jesus the Christ. He is a person, individually distinct from the Father, but closely related. He has great intelligence and can understand and operate cosmic energies. He is profoundly compassionate and sympathetic but emotionally balanced. All His senses are acutely developed. He has X-ray sight; ears that can hear every octave of sound. His body can both transmit and receive on cosmic wavelength, to the Father God or to His human comrades with equal facility for in His blood is all record of experience. He is master of detail. All this is without effort on His part. He is always in Love and no effort is entailed in being in love. There is no virtue in loving, there is no virtue in oiling a machine, but it is sheer folly to let it rust for lack of oil. It is sheer folly not to love. Life becomes dirty and gritty and out of these sordid substances pessimism is born.

Jesus is the greatest lover of all times; the greatest scientist, biologist, explorer, orator. His legal mind was a match for the trained deceptionists. His *joie de vivre* was an infection. His health contagious for His very garments gave it out. His love of little children was great, His love for His Father transcended all other emotion. If He had not known the Father He could not have had faith. Faith is the substance of experience. What faith the disciples achieved was derived from their individual experience of friendship with Jesus. What faith we achieve will depend on our individual experience. We can get it in no other way. We can neither borrow, buy or imitate it. It can never be stolen or commandeered. No human experience separated Jesus from the Father save death. It was to overcome that separation that He incarnated. What an adventure for Him, what an adventure for us.

PART II

THE CHRISTIAN INITIATION

There is a way for those who want to follow in Christ's footsteps along the path of reconstruction and are willing to give up their lives to bring about peace on earth. To give up one's life is not to die, but to surrender habit of thought. It is the experience of dying to oneself and living for one's neighbour. Peace is the exact opposite of war and just as dynamic; to live for one's neighbour instead of killing him needs often greater courage and endurance and cannot be done merely by taking thought. Jesus was not a contemplative. He was an executive. Thought and action in Him became simultaneous. He was the Light. He worked with the speed of Light, "He lifted up His eyes," and in that moment the miracle happened. He became the law of creative energy in visible manifestation. His body was the perfect instrument.

The Technique in Light was given to bring about the same condition in our bodies as He achieved in His. He started with no sin, no expiation, no need for forgiveness. We all start heavily handicapped with karmic bondage. The action of the cosmic rays on matter is to quicken it into activity; the more concentrated, the greater the result. Jesus learnt in 33 years to draw in the maximum amount that flesh and blood can absorb. The disciples, like ourselves, had much to eliminate, much to change, and they could only draw from Him what each could absorb. Paul of Tarsus, after his stupendous experience, learnt to focus his mind on the mind of Christ and though he was never able to free himself entirely from his physical disabilities, he was able to transcend his infirmities to a remarkable degree. Paul was filled with a fervent desire to co-ordinate the dual nature of the average man, which is the natural desire to do the wrong thing contending with the spiritual urge towards freedom from mental strife. Peace of mind is the peace that the world cannot give.

The disciples in their generation had a work to do, which they did magnificently. They taught the truth of the reconstruction of the body and

The Christian Initiation

recorded facts concerning the re-appearance of the physical body of Jesus and how it operated. They became fearless of public opinion; their courage of living was the courage of love.

In our generation we have a work to do. We have to re-represent Christ to the world; we have to take Him down from the cross and give Him the opportunity to direct the peace proposals for world freedom. It can only be brought about by individual effort. There is so much unco-ordinated goodwill. Without action, goodwill goes bad. Without direction, activity can be harmful.

The difficulties that beset an undedicated man of goodwill are very great. To a dedicated man there are no difficulties. That may seem an overstatement, but it is not. There were no difficulties in Christ's life; every crisis was immediately surrendered; the direction given and taken; the responsibility lifted; serenity established.

The Christian Initiation is a technique to enable the ordinary person, man, woman or child, of any class, race or creed, to learn how to open the mind to receive revealed knowledge, direct from the mind of Christ. Step by step the self is revealed, the veils of illusion are gently removed and capacity is reborn. Capacity to become a Christ; not to think but to receive thought; not to be emotional, but to tune into Love and to identify oneself with Love. Not to speculate how Jesus would function in the 20th century, but to learn how He can direct individual life, how He can inspire the mind to solve the insoluble problems of the modern world. We, Christian Initiates, know that it can be done. We know through experience that the human body can be transformed into an instrument of receptivity and transmission of eternal life energy. We know, because we are very ordinary people and the works that have been done through us have not been done by us. We have proved that the Technique in Light is an exact formula of revelation; that it is a process which produces a chemical change in the body and an unending expansion of mind. We are like children, knowing nothing of science, biology or research, but we can receive in a flash knowledge that might take a lifetime to acquire.

We have learnt that the brain is the receiving set, that the blood is the transmitting agent, and that given the true focus of the mind, the physical reaction is definite. Once the child learns the alphabet, reading then becomes a matter of application and of diligence. Once we learn the Technique in Light, channelhood is an inevitable result, but application and faithfulness are necessary to achieve the Christ standard. I use the word "channel" rather than healer, for though Jesus healed, He was the channel through whom the Father manifested.

The Technique in Light is the method by which the process of turning the ordinary person into a channel is accomplished. A channel through whom the Christ can transmit eternal energy. We in our generation can be given a far more exact understanding than could be given two thousand years ago. There was so much that He wanted to impart of truth, but He knew well that their brains then could not absorb any more. He has had to wait until the modern mind, trained in mechanical processes, can receive the understanding.

Men have exteriorised the human mechanism into wireless and television instruments. They have also classified certain cosmic rays such as X-ray, infra-red ray and made instruments to demonstrate their working power. Jesus tried to teach the world how to receive into their own person those very rays for curative action. He received and transmitted them and He wanted everyone to learn how to receive them direct. The same difficulty occurs today that He was faced with then. The resisting power of the human mind. Human beings want miracles done for them, they cannot believe that they can learn how miracles can be done through them.

The Technique in Light teaches us our capacity for the fourth dimensional activity of "throughness". We learn that when the mind is focused on the Christ, a happening takes place with no effort on our part. We do not think it a miracle when we plug a lampstand into the wall and the lamp is illuminated; on the contrary, we would know that something was wrong if it did not shine. The Christian Initiate learns it is a universal condition that when we plug our minds into the mind of Christ, the

The Christian Initiation

knowledge needed is received. If it is not received it is because the instrument is out of order.

The Technique in Light teaches us that visualising Light identifies us with the substance of Light and attracts it to us. We have learnt that in the pineal gland is a magnetic point which enables every living person to see, to visualise, or to imagine mental pictures. It is our television set. The Father was able to transmit the true pattern into Christ's mind, because His television apparatus was always tuned in to the Father. Christ knew that it was expedient for Him to return to the world of cosmic harmony in order to be able to transmit to the disciples during their lifetime, the true pattern of human capacity. It could only be accomplished if He could impress on them the urgent need for remembrance. We Christian Initiates know that to be true. Nothing can happen through us, unless our mind holds His. Directly the mind travels back to worldly conditions the contact is cut and a dimension is dropped.

Every exercise in the Technique is designed to start the process of reconstruction, or resurrection of the physical instrument. The process of decay in the mind is caused by the gradual insulation of the mind, by the acceptance of a mystical body of Christ instead of an eternally human one. It is logical to assume that if Christ lost His humanity when He returned to the Father, then we too must lose our humanity when we die, death retaining its sting and the grave its victory.

We know, through our experience, that Jesus made human substance eternal, unchangeably the same, as in fact it was in the beginning; in Him it is now the same and ever shall be. Decay is the receding of the life force in matter. Death is the total absence of life energy. Connect up the decaying substance with life, and transmutation takes place and that which was dying becomes vitalised. Human substance that never decays and never dies is the basic condition of life in cosmic harmony, the heaven of human aspiration. Jesus came to establish cosmic harmony on earth. He reiterated again and again that the functioning power was in the heart and until the heart activity was in motion, no true result could be obtained. The brain is incapable of receiving more than the pattern of the law, the heart must put it into living activity. Thus the whole body becomes involved in the experience.

Jesus incarnated to earth perfect human receptivity. He returned to heaven to demonstrate the broadcasting system that operates in cosmic harmony. Short circuiting in electrical energy causes a fuse in the apparatus. Jesus could not make use of electrical symbolism, He could only compare eternal life to oil lamps; the fertilising of seed; lightning, "As the lightning flashes from the east even unto the west, so shall the coming of the Son of MAN be." He so demonstrates the earthing of the cosmic rays in flesh and blood must function as Light functions, IS the Light, and therefore will travel with the speed of Light, will flash from east to west. The detonation of such a happening will fill the heavens with the sound of it. Creative energy has a sound that man has never heard. Destructive energy has a noise that man will never forget.

The Technique in Light is a preparation for living experience, all science is embodied in it. Every man can receive truth along his own professional activity, but every man must learn to distinguish between need for knowledge and the desire for knowledge. Need is the magnetic attraction that draws truth. Desire has no magnetic power. If we had X-ray eyes, we should see how the life currents are attracted or repelled by thought wavelengths. When the heart and the brain become aware of a neighbour's need, the capacity of the instrument to receive the supply to satisfy the need is put into operation and the supply is inevitably given. On the other hand, when the desire to acquire is urgently demanded, there is little or no magnetic force, and the demand is often inoperative. It does not travel on cosmic wavelength to harmony but is short-circuited and fusing takes place in the instrument. Asking to supply another's need is a dominant heart action. Desire to have for oneself is a cerebral action and has no travelling power, does not reach the Source, but has to depend on human will power. The dependence on human will power and mental control is the basic cause of death and disease of physical substance. "Not my will but Thine be done, on earth as it is in heaven," is the law of cosmic harmony.

The Christian Initiation

It is the mistaken idea of the average person that it is good to develop the human will power; that to be strong minded is to be great minded. It is not so.

The Technique in Light teaches us how to receive thought instead of thinking. It changes the destructive energy of the comparative, competitive and critical faculties. No Christian Initiate can compare themselves with another Christian Initiate; no comparison is possible. If one can receive the Christ's life force, it cannot be a competitive condition; it is a sharing and we all have equal capacity to receive and share Him. If comparisons are made, if distinctions are insisted on, it is a mark of ignorance, the hallmark of third dimensional minds. In the mind of Christ and the Father God are no distinctions, only the recognition of unity.

The Technique in Light teaches us the power of unity. How simple it is to become the Light. Visualise Light and the sparking process starts. The Christian Initiate cannot meditate and must not separate thought from action. The Lord's prayer is the perfect example of Christ's endeavour to teach people how prayer operates. First the focus of the mind on the universal "Our Father who art in Harmony. Hallowed be Thy Name," the focal point is thus established. The object of focusing the mind on the Father is now disclosed, the whole of Christ's mission made clear. "Thy kingdom come", - cosmic harmony. "Thy will be done on earth as it is in Harmony"; that implies unconditional surrender of the human will resulting in eternal activity.

Since He has said that no active change can be wrought by "taking thought," it seems odd that people believe that meditation will bring about physical reconstruction. God's will operating on earth through mankind must change the earth into cosmic harmony.

The Christian Initiate realises that God created matter, therefore He is the expert on all material conditions. The first request, "Give us this day our daily bread," reveals the foundation of Christ's miracles, the need for physical substance supplied daily and asked for daily. When we have learnt how to ask, the supply is inevitably given. Christ realised how the subtle mind works: if God knows what we want, why cannot He give us what we want without asking? Jesus knew that simplicity of approach produces instant results. The subtle mind cannot make a direct contact and cannot receive an instant response.

"Forgive us our trespasses as we forgive them that trespass against us." Forgiveness is a dynamic activity, not a cerebral condition. I know people who meditate on forgiveness, yet never forgive. Recognising in oneself the hateful activity of jealousy, possessiveness, fear or pride is to ensure in oneself the capacity to forgive. It may take a lifetime, it probably has taken many, but Jesus knew that if only He could get across the barrier of resistance and make the people understand that individual responsibility must be accepted for every action and every word uttered and must not be placed on circumstances or people, then and then only could forgiveness be asked for and forgiveness be given.

"Let us not be led into temptation." Again there is the need for focus, the necessity for discernment of spirit in order to clarify the mind from mixed motives and to receive the divine direction.

We know that the action of Light is instantaneous. Jesus knew it too. The speed of thought is immeasurable, so is the spark of our mind to Christ's mind to ask for direction; immediately thought and action become simultaneous.

"Deliver us from evil." What activity is involved in that one sentence. When danger threatens us, of what use is it to try to find a church and kneel in prayer? One must learn to spark every minute of every day if one is not to be led astray and if every danger that threatens us is averted. Without the activity of prayer we are helpless, for "Thine is the power, the strength and the glory."

The radio-activity of the Father who talks of His children as the children of Light in contrast to the children of bondage, is a condition of revelation and exhilaration to the Christian Initiate. From the very beginning the human race was created to replenish the earth with the life force which they were capable of receiving into their blood and transmitting through their hands and feet. We shall have a new earth

The Christian Initiation

when we learn how to replenish it instead of interring our diseased bodies and contaminating the soil for future generations. No wonder Shakespeare thought that only the evil in man lived after him with so much evidence to support such a terrible accusation.

Can our mortality be changed into immortality by just visualising Light? The act of visualising the different substances of Light on the body is the way that contact is made. We have an organ of identification, the inner eye or pineal gland; with that organ we have an unused capacity for functioning power. By it we can see the transcendental and record it on periscopic lines. The Technique in Light develops the consciousness of the individual. One becomes aware of invisible matter, certain faculties of touch and hearing long rusted through lack of use in many lives, are brought again into activity through daily exercises in the visualising of the cosmic rays.

Now Christians may wonder, if Light is a universal source of life, why must all the world receive it only through the Christ's body? Why cannot people draw it quite simply from the universal supply? Radium is also a universal substance, but if it had remained in its original condition and Madame Curie had not made it her life's mission to learn how to extract it, and thus give the world its use, humanity could not have benefited. It is the same with the cosmic rays. If Christ had not incarnated to show humanity how to receive and transmit the life energy, if He had not experimented on His own body first, humanity could never, through instinct alone, have become harmonised with cosmic energy. If it were merely a mental conception of cosmic harmony, then indeed Plato, Confucius, Buddha or Mohammed held equal places as teachers of truth. But Christ is the only living exponent of eternal life, and therefore unless we tap the mind of the expert we shall never know the truth. To know how a thing should be done is one thing; to be able to do it is another. One has to learn the technique of any profession before one can master it.

When one starts learning how to function in a new dimension, one has to acquire a new habit of thought. That new habit is to stop thinking and allow Christ to broadcast into our minds. The Light exercises train the

the mind to focus on Him and each exercise is designed to release the energy to flow to every part of the body. Our bodies are the manifestation of our minds. If we can achieve the mind of Christ, our bodies will be transformed and made "like unto His glorious body".

The objection is often raised as to why this insistence on bodily perfection is so important, and are there not so many beautiful minds housed in sick and frail bodies, and is not suffering a necessary condition of spiritual progress. It is perfectly true that many good people are hopeless invalids and bear their cross patiently and bravely. That does not invalidate their capacity to have a beautiful mind *and* a beautiful body. It is an instance of the separation of the individual, the acceptance of mental life energy, the placing of Christ's body on the mystical plane which vitalises the visionary activity but devitalises the physical energy.

The summit of achievement of the old worships of Light was the illumination of the mind. Christ illuminated the blood. The object of the Technique in Light is to bring it again into universal circulation, without suffering. He suffered vicariously to bring about the release of human capacity, that we who deserve to suffer might find this way which sparks us back to Love's harmony. All suffering is caused by this separation of mental focus, by our identifying ourselves with the salutary effect of suffering. It is the means which the human race has chosen to try and effect the end they have in view.

Christ came to establish another route, whereby tears would be a thing of the past, where the road would be so brilliantly lit that no stumbling blocks could be put on the path. No agent save Light can transcend darkness.

Christ used no scientific terms of distinction between Light and energy. He taught the disciples through experience, how eternal life was received and transmitted. If they followed His instructions they were safe. He knew that every human instrument is fitted with a safety catch, and that safety device is the heart.

I have often been asked why I associated the Technique in Light with the Christian Initiation, since Christ never left a technique to guide

The Christian Initiation

His disciples. When I started receiving on my television set (i.e. pineal gland) the pattern of the Technique and at the same time received the understanding that I was to identify my own body with the exercises given, I was totally unaware that it was not an individual experience.

Obediently I followed my daily directions. My body responded and very gradually the pattern developed and the living instrument became aware of a new capacity. I found my hands could receive the radiations transmitted by wood and stone. Those radiations sparked into my television apparatus pictures of happenings absorbed by the receptive action of the substance my fingers touched. By degrees an accurate condition of receptivity and transmission was established. The action of the Light exercises released the freedom of my hands. Still I did not realise that it was anything but a thrilling individual experience. The training continued and slowly it was borne in on me that it was the exercises which caused the change. A few people started doing them, and my eyes were opened and I saw. I saw that fear could be eliminated through daily contact with Christ's living blood radiation. I was made to realise, through many hard experiences, why it was intermittent, why it acted sometimes with so little effort and why, when the urgency was great, the failure was so complete.

The Light exercises exposed all the hidden motives which governed one's actions, it made one aware of one's fatal facility for inaccurate statement in ordinary conversation, and what an uncontrolled organ the tongue can be. Each time that my awareness of my own weakness was recognised, an exercise was given, a certain substance of Light was revealed as an antidote, and if the directions were faithfully followed, a change took place and one was given strength when the need for it occurred. I recognised that failure was the result of the slack working of the instrument and not due to the energy that set it in motion. I was determined to recondition the instrument. That determination is still in process.

It was a very long time, years in fact, before those of us who started on this path of reconditioning realised our objective, which was not just to remain a Christian, but to become a Christ. We realised that we were channels through whom Christ could function intermittently, but what He really wanted to accomplish through us was mercifully hidden until we were able to bear it. To achieve the Christ's standard of efficiency, to be able to do the things needed in our generation as He supplied the need of His generation, involves special training. He taught His disciples then by a method that He alone was able to teach, that of personal demonstration, and the result of that personal daily training has never been achieved since. The Church they started was founded on personal experience, on devoted service to humanity, on utter selflessness and singleness of purpose. The people believed the stupendous story they told of the resurrection and ascension of the man Jesus, crucified and buried according to Roman regulations. The Church was a living demonstration of a living contact with a living Christ. Works directly inspired were the foundation stone of the early Church.

If we are to have a new Church, it must start by having a new foundation stone, and in place of the letter of the Law, the living heart of the Prince of Peace; in that heart the nations will unite.

I have been accused of drawing a picture of the millennium. Is it not about time that we had a diagram of the millennium and started working on it? How can the world change be brought about when one cannot get the modicum of agreement in home politics or international finance? My answer to the pessimists is "How is bread made? What is the substance absolutely necessary for good baking? Leaven!" Just that one word, 'leaven'. We Christian Initiates must give up our lives to produce the substance that will leaven the world disharmony. The leaven of Love will change the whole substance of mammon.

Each mind and every nation that puts financial security before human need, sows the seed of internal and international strife. Each mind and every nation that puts human need before financial security, sows the seed of personal and international prosperity. It is not wishful thinking or a great ideal but it is a common law.

The great love Christ had for children was based on His need for

The Christian Initiation

their co-operation. The sensitiveness of a child's mind, its natural receptivity was the material He need to demonstrate the magnetic power of love. The Scribes and Pharisees with their erudite and academic minds had to have the most drastic lesson to penetrate their armour of pride and self-sufficiency. The receptive mind of a child that is aware that it does not know what the grown-ups know, was the perfect example needed for His training of the disciples. The child's type of mind has no mental resistance, and has greater capacity to receive than the mind which is filled with acquired knowledge. For that mind it is difficult to hold a new understanding, since it involves the emptying of the substance acquired through long years and lives of diligence. To the adult it was an unthink-able proposition, only a madman could propound so preposterous a demand. The child also represented the new generation and we are told again and again that the contact Jesus made with children was on their heads. He put His wonderful hands on their heads and an injection of eternal energy was given, that was the blessing He always bestowed. It is my firm conviction that all great leaders of progressive spiritual movements, in all the ages, made a contact with Jesus two thousand years ago.

Much of the difficulty experienced by parents in teaching religious truth to children would be eliminated if the parents did the Technique. They would find that the children drew through them what they needed to know. They would also find that children could visualise quite easily and fascinating games could be devised for them. Parents would also find that one cannot give what one is not prepared to receive. Doctors can prescribe medicines for their patients that they would never dream of taking themselves, but parents cannot give truth to their children unless they are prepared to receive it first. One cannot live to oneself however hard one tries. It is definitely a childish trait to want to know the truth about everything; when we are grown up it is often the last thing we want to know for we have an inherent fear that it is bound to be unpleasant.

Fear! How ashamed and rightly ashamed we are of our fears and how we camouflage them to ourselves and to the world. Fear reacts differently in everybody, and although we may have the same brand of fear ranging from ghosts to burglars, the individual reaction to any or all brands differs greatly in degree.

Fear is cerebral, the reaction is physical. All disease can be traced back to fear for fear is the origin of sin; disease is the reaction of sin. Jesus came to take away our sin, to wash it away in His blood. Unless we understand the cosmic law, the reiteration of cleansing by blood becomes a nauseating repetition of an act which as a child, I found completely revolting. I was of the generation of the child who was heard to say to the nurse outside the drawing room door. "Tumpany or no tumpany, I won't have my face washed in spit!" I made a similar determination, sin or no sin, I was never going to be washed in blood. If I had known as a child that blood was Light, that the Light shining out from the blood of Jesus was like a wonderful ruby which could light me up the stairs in the dark, that if I thought of Him instead of watching the darkness, then going to bed at night could have become a very different experience.

Darkness can never lose its terrors until we learn our power to receive the Light, nor can we lose fear until through experience of the working power of Light, it is replaced by confidence. Confidence in Christ's power to transmit life energy is the same as faith. Faith is the substance of experience and without experience there can be no faith, only hope. Hope is the pattern of experience, faith is the substance of it. I want to stress that, for so many people say they have lost their faith or that they have not any, and such people are totally unaware of what faith is. They think it is believing in the reality of the invisible, and frankly they cannot. Of course they cannot. I believe and have faith in nothing that I myself have not experienced. I have hope that I shall accomplish and a great desire to finish my job, and I have complete confidence in my senior partner, Jesus Christ, but there is no faith or confidence in myself. All my experience proves that however hard I try, the things I want to do I cannot achieve, and that which is needed to be done, however difficult

The Christian Initiation

and impossible it looks, can be done easily and with no effort through me, by my Senior Partner. That is my faith which I cannot possibly lose.

Christian faith is experience of contact with Christ and those people who have ever had it, have always got it. Anybody who has ever had a contact with an exposed electric wire can never lose that experience, for they know for all time what it feels like.

It is perfectly true that thousands of people who are classified as Christians have no knowledge of Christ as a divinely human companion, but they could find their way in their particular prayer book and in the Old Testament. They may have knowledge of church history but no intimacy or co-operation of works with its Founder. No longer must we remain ignorant of the distinction that exists between the works of the church and the works of Christ, and between the ecclesiastical mind and the mind of Christ. Which is the first loyalty and which is the second? Is it to the Founder or to the organisation? Is it to the Master or to His stewards? Each individual who believes himself or herself to be a Christian must answer those questions according to the integrity of their mind. Each priest must also ask himself the true origin of his vocation to represent the living Christ; whether it is love or expediency, whether he can perform the works of Christ or only preach about them.

The capacity to represent Christ on earth is given to all men and all women. Jesus made no distinction, therefore the responsibility is universal as well as individual.

The Technique in Light is a method given to our generation to bring into being the Order of the New Covenant, when no man shall teach his brother, but that all people shall know Him, from the least unto the greatest. No one is left out of that great Order, the unit of world service. He sketched out the plan 2,000 years ago, for He knew that He would never be able to manifest again as a man until all religious controversies ended, until the Law was written in flesh and blood, in the organs and in hearts, until there was one Church, the Church of the Resurrection. In that Church He will officiate. He will give us His body and His blood. He will commune with us. He will operate the law of transubstantiation and out of the love in our hearts He will materialise. When?

That depends on you and me. Can we give our bodies as He gave His? Can we surrender our wills as He surrendered His? Can we start again with the enthusiasm of a little child? Can we give our time, the only gift that is exclusively ours to give? Will He accept our inferiority complex, our exclusiveness, our fear of appearing ridiculous? Can He rid us of our past? Can He? Of course He can. Though our fears are bright scarlet, He can transmute them into the brilliant whiteness of the Father's will. He is an expert transmuter, changing one substance into another, knowing the exact amount of energy to use for each attribute, till fear becomes confidence, pride changes to humility, ignorance into comprehension. He knows what each character needs in the way of stimulus or discipline.

It is not a question of time. It can be done in our lifetime, but whether it will or not depends on us and not on Him. We live in time, He does not. Time matters to us, it does not matter to Him. He is time. When we tune in to Him we become Him for that moment. If we learn through the action of Light to become Light, then we must attract Him to us. If there are enough of us to attract Him, then He must come. He gave the minimum when He said that two or three tuning in to Him attracted Him to them. Anyone who has had that experience knows it to be true; those who have not cannot know it. What a person does not know is no concern of the person who does know. If anybody asks for knowledge they can never be refused by Christ or by a Christian Initiate. "Ask and ye shall receive." In modern terms we translate "ask" into "tuning in" or "making contact", and the result is as inevitable as the striking of a match to make a flame. If the match is damp, there is no flame. If we do not know how to tune in because we have lost the faculty for doing so, then the verbal request from an unconfident mind brings about a very feeble result. A verbal request from an absolutely confident mind makes a contact through the substance of confidence, not in uttering the word. The explosion of sound through the mouth has no cosmic carrying power without the confidence from the heart; the ray of light making a contact

The Christian Initiation

with the light in the blood has the travelling power and carries the request in Light to Light.

We know through the training in Light how prayer operates. It is a sparking process and there is a great rejoicing at G.H.Q. when the request for help sparks through the traffic lights of the mental and astral suburbs right into the heart of the city, where a competent organisation immediately deals with the request. Earth laws are modelled on those that operate in heaven or harmony. I think the reason why heaven has little appeal for business men is that they imagine it to be a place where nothing is solid or tangible and therefore too uncomfortable as a permanent residence. They want to stick to the good old earth as long as they can, where at least a man can have a run for his money, and who knows what happens when one cannot tip one's way about?

As a matter of fact it is a very tangible solid place. We have learnt that Light in the world of Light is as solid as matter is on earth. Light can pass through matter, but Light does not pass through Light. There are as many different substances in Light as there are in matter. All earthly form is inspired by form in Light. No artist or architect is ever really satisfied with the concrete form of his inspiration. There is a quality that he can never quite materialise. That quality he will see reproduced in Light substance when he returns to harmony from whence his earthly mind received its inspiration.

Our soul bodies are as solid in Light as our physical bodies are solid in matter, so it is not wise to lay up all our treasure on earth. We feel a bit naked when we take our better half over the border and have to leave all our possessions and our lesser half behind. I wonder how many people feel, as my brother felt when he was catapulted over during the last war — "What a fool I've been not to find out, when I had the capacity, how to function over here." There is a certain glamour in lawlessness but none in foolishness and when one recognises that in breaking the law one automatically becomes a fool, the desire to break the law vanishes very speedily. The fool becomes wise, but the fool must realise that he has to become wise in this world if he wants to function happily and prosperously in heaven. Investment in Light takes place on earth, the dividends alone being paid in heaven.

This document has been written for the purpose making known a method which was received through revelation ten years ago and which has been faithfully applied. It was not known what the results would be, it could only be a matter of experience. Those experiences proved that when the Technique in Light was followed with singleness of purpose and integrity of mind, channelhood was the inevitable result. Then the healing started and we did not realise where these first beginnings were to lead us. "Those to whom much is given of these much is required." Therefore the self revelation became much more searching, the dregs in the bottle that had to be prepared to hold the new wine without breaking, had to be cleared out. This dredging process has gone on steadily during the years of war and as the dregs disappear and the wine seeps in, the exhilaration is intense and sharing becomes necessary.

At the end of the last war we kept a light shining by the grave of the unknown soldier. To light a lamp in memory of the dead is to keep the memory eternally alive. Now a greater thing is asked of us and that is to *become* the Light. The body is the lamp or the temple; the blood absorbs the Light. Let our blood shine so that the works Christ did 2,000 years ago may be done again. Other works, because of greater opportunity and greater need, demand an expanding scale. Let us not put a limit on His activity either in time or space. Wherever we are, if we learn how to ask, we shall receive. No more fear, no more pessimism, for the former things will pass away, and when the Light flashes from the east to the west, we, with our lamps shining, will be here to welcome the Son of Man.

Postscript

Having read the narratives and should the reader now
genuinely wish to follow in the path of the Christian Initiate
and learn how to *become* the Light,
the Technique, as it was revealed to Olive Pixley,
is recorded in a short series of books.

Each book, which is essentially a manual of exercises and talks,
takes the reader through the training in Light in progressively
the same manner as Olive Pixley experienced.
In order of progression these are:-

The Armour of Light - Part I
Revised Edition comprising Volumes I and II

The Armour of Light - Part II

The Magnet

All publications may be purchased from:-

The Armour of Light Trust Council
Irena Dean
11 Pathfields
Shere
Surrey GU5 9HP
England
Tel/Fax: 01483 202701